Charles Taylor

The Witness of Hermas to the Four Gospels

Charles Taylor

The Witness of Hermas to the Four Gospels

ISBN/EAN: 9783337281007

Printed in Europe, USA, Canada, Australia, Japan

Cover: Foto ©Lupo / pixelio.de

More available books at **www.hansebooks.com**

THE
WITNESS OF HERMAS

TO

THE FOUR GOSPELS

BY

C. TAYLOR D.D.

MASTER OF ST JOHN'S COLLEGE CAMBRIDGE

LONDON
C. J. CLAY AND SONS
CAMBRIDGE UNIVERSITY PRESS WAREHOUSE
AVE MARIA LANE
1892

[*All Rights reserved*]

PREFACE

THE *Shepherd of Hermas* is an incompletely worked mine of allusions to the Gospels and other writings. It has been undervalued because it has not been understood. In form it is a lengthy revelation to one Hermas, written down by himself; but while some take his story for history, perhaps more deem it an offspring of the imagination, and place it in the same category with the famous *Pilgrim's Progress*. Its author, who has a sufficiency of sacred and secular lore at command, never cites by name, except once from the now lost *Eldad and Modat*, but weaves his materials artfully together into a fabric which must be unravelled with some care before it can be seen of what elements it is composed.

The *Witness of Hermas to the Four Gospels* is an incidental result of a detailed study of the *Shepherd* in relation to the *Teaching of the Twelve Apostles* for the purpose of deciding which of the two writings borrowed from the other. And first it seemed to come out clearly that Hermas had many covert allusions to the *Teaching*; and next that his use of it was so comprehensive that the best method of comparison was to read through the *Teaching*, note things at all remarkable in it, and search for hidden traces of them in the *Shepherd*. By this *a priori* method I was led to anticipate the discovery of the word Gospel under some disguise in the work of Hermas, and I found it in the form ἀγγελία ἀγαθή, *Good Tidings*.

A singular illustration in the context is usually left unexplained, and has been thought to have no meaning; but as soon as it was seen that the Gospel was referred to (as was not unnatural at the end of the third apparition of the Church to Hermas) it became possible to interpret the passage in the light of the doctrine of Irenaeus, that from the nature of things there can be neither more nor fewer than four true Gospels, because "when God has made all things compounded and fitted together, the form of the Gospel too must needs have been well compounded and compacted." Taking for granted and as known to all that the universe was compounded of a tetrad of elements, he infers that the complete Gospel must have been made up of a tetrad of Gospels. When therefore Hermas writes in his chapter on the Good Tidings, "for the world also is compacted of four elements," he would have us know that it was recognised in his day in the metropolis of the Empire that the Canonical Gospels were four in number.

For the date of the *Shepherd of Hermas* the Muratorian fragment gives approximately the limits 140—150 A.D.; and we may say that, even if the work was finished only toward the end of the period named, its testimony would still go back to not far from 140 A.D., since the idea of so extensive and elaborate a composition must have been already for some time in the mind of the writer. Not having encountered any obstacle to acquiescence in the Muratorian date of the *Shepherd* in the course of my comparisons of it with other writings, I am content to accept that date provisionally, without denying that there are considerations, urged by weighty authorities, which seem to shew that Hermas may have written somewhat earlier. In any case, if the argument of this essay be sound, the Four Gospels have been shewn to have attained to their exclusive and canonical position a third of a century or more before Irenaeus made his statement that there were, and could not but have been, four "Gospels of the Apostles" and four only.

borrowed from the other. And first it seemed to come out clearly that Hermas had many covert allusions to the *Teaching*; and next that his use of it was so comprehensive that the best method of comparison was to read through the *Teaching*, note things at all remarkable in it, and search for hidden traces of them in the *Shepherd*. By this *a priori* method I was led to anticipate the discovery of the word Gospel under some disguise in the work of Hermas, and I found it in the form ἀγγελία ἀγαθή, *Good Tidings*.

A singular illustration in the context is usually left unexplained, and has been thought to have no meaning; but as soon as it was seen that the Gospel was referred to (as was not unnatural at the end of the third apparition of the Church to Hermas) it became possible to interpret the passage in the light of the doctrine of Irenaeus, that from the nature of things there can be neither more nor fewer than four true Gospels, because "when God has made all things compounded and fitted together, the form of the Gospel too must needs have been well compounded and compacted." Taking for granted and as known to all that the universe was compounded of a tetrad of elements, he infers that the complete Gospel must have been made up of a tetrad of Gospels. When therefore Hermas writes in his chapter on the Good Tidings, "for the world also is compacted of four elements," he would have us know that it was recognised in his day in the metropolis of the Empire that the Canonical Gospels were four in number.

For the date of the *Shepherd of Hermas* the Muratorian fragment gives approximately the limits 140—150 A.D.; and we may say that, even if the work was finished only toward the end of the period named, its testimony would still go back to not far from 140 A.D., since the idea of so extensive and elaborate a composition must have been already for some time in the mind of the writer. Not having encountered any obstacle to acquiescence in the Muratorian date of the *Shepherd* in the course of my comparisons of it with other writings, I am content to accept that date provisionally, without denying that there are considerations, urged by weighty authorities, which seem to shew that Hermas may have written somewhat earlier. In any case, if the argument of this essay be sound, the Four Gospels have been shewn to have attained to their exclusive and canonical position a third of a century or more before Irenaeus made his statement that there were, and could not but have been, four "Gospels of the Apostles" and four only.

The proof that Hermas prefigured this dictum of Irenaeus is followed by a search for traces of the Gospels in the *Shepherd*, which is in the main a fresh enquiry; but I have profited by the perusal of Zahn's kindred study in *Der Hirt des Hermas* (1868), and have used Hilgenfeld's *Hermae Pastor* (1881) as a summary of the conclusions of exegetes from Cotelier to Harnack and Funk. For suggestive criticism and counsel in the final revision I am indebted to the learning and judgment of Dr Sanday. At an earlier stage I had, with much advantage, discussed some dubious points with Dr Gifford.

Notes of the essay were read at Sion College on the 22nd October 1891 and shortly afterwards in Cambridge. Two years previously I had written of Irenaeus that "his analogies for the necessity of there being Four Gospels must have been suggested by Hermas."

C. TAYLOR

CAMBRIDGE
25th March 1892

I.

HERMAS

AND

THE FOUR GOSPELS.

ΟΥΔΕΝ ΓΑΡ ΚΕΝΟΝ ΟΥΔΕ ΑΣΥΜΒΟΛΟΝ

HERMAS AND THE FOUR GOSPELS.

THE late Bishop of Durham, in his volume of replies to the book *Supernatural Religion*, gives this summary of the early evidence for the Gospels at the end of the essay on the Churches of Gaul (p. 271):

One other remark on the testimony of Irenaeus suggests itself before closing. Irenaeus is the first extant writer in whom, from the nature of his work, we have a right to expect explicit information on the subject of the Canon. Earlier writings, which have been preserved entire, are either epistolary, like the letters of the Apostolic Fathers, where any references to the Canonical books must necessarily be precarious and incidental (to say nothing of the continuance of the oral tradition at this date as a disturbing element); or devotional, like the Shepherd of Hermas, which is equally devoid of citations from the Old Testament and the New; or historical, like the account of the martyrdoms at Vienne and Lyons, where any such allusion is gratuitous; or apologetic, like the great mass of the extant Christian writings of the second century, where the reserve of the writer naturally leads him to be silent about authorities which would carry no weight with the Jewish or heathen readers whom he addressed. But the work of Irenaeus is the first controversial treatise addressed to Christians on questions of Christian doctrine, where the appeal lies to Christian documents. And here the testimony to our four Gospels is full and clear and precise.

It is a prevalent opinion that the work of Hermas is of little or no value for the history of the Canon. But I have been led to think that its testimony, especially to the Gospels, is strong and convincing, although it does not lie on the surface: that it says in effect that the number of the Gospels was actually and necessarily four, as Irenaeus said after it: and that Irenaeus was indebted to Hermas in respect of that important and remarkable statement, for which the later writer is always taken to be the independent and original authority.

1. *Hermas.*

I said that I had been led to think that Hermas has something of great value to tell us about the Gospels; and I meant by this that I had been led on step by step by train of argument to a conclusion which was as unexpected as it was unsought. I was not thinking of any moot point in the history of the Canon, but only of the relation of the *Teaching of the Twelve Apostles* to the *Shepherd of Hermas*. I was writing an article on this for the *Journal of Philology*, and had satisfied myself that Hermas not only used, but used up the *Teaching;* so that anything very striking in that manual had only to be looked for in the *Shepherd*, and there it would in due course be found in one disguise or other*. Coming near to the end of the comparison of the two writings, I was considering the words in the last chapter but one of the *Teaching*, "And your prayers and your alms and all that ye do, so do as ye have it in the Gospel of our Lord," when it occurred to me that there ought to be some trace of the word Gospel in Hermas.

---

* The method of Hermas is to some extent shewn below by examples independent of the Gospels in the preamble of the section on *Hermas and the Synoptic Gospels*.

I set to work to read through the *Shepherd* for the purpose of finding in it a disguised trace of the word εὐαγγέλιον, *gospel.* I came to *Vis.* iii. 13. 2, and found ἀγγελία ἀγαθή, *good tidings,* which was evidently the thing sought. Then at once it seemed clear to me, in the light of sayings of Irenaeus which will be quoted below, that under the figure of the bench (συμψέλιον*) standing firmly on four feet, in the immediate context, Hermas refers to the Four Gospels, comparing them to the four elements of the world. Thus a meaning was found where apparently none had been found before; for the fullest commentary on the *Shepherd,* with all the learning of all previous commentators at its back, has nothing to add here to the laconic sentence of a contemporary, *Argumentatio mere inepta,* it is mere nonsense.

The passage in question is the peroration of the account of the Church's appearances to Hermas in three successive forms:

In *Vis.* i. she was an aged woman who sat alone upon a great white *chair* of snowy wools (2. 2) and read from a book to Hermas. When she had done reading she rose from the chair, and four young men

---

* The word is from the Latin *subsellium.* In Rabbinic Hebrew it takes the form *safsal.* On the bench see also *Mand.* xi.

came and carried it off to the East, and two others carried her to the same place (4. 1, 3). The word for chair or seat is that used in the saying, *The scribes sit in Moses' seat*, and it denotes also an easy chair suited for a sick person. The Church accordingly both teaches from it *ex cathedra*, and (as we shall see) reclines upon it as sick and at the point of death.

In *Vis*. ii. she is seen walking and reading a little book (1. 3). Hermas mistakes her for the Sibyl, but is told that she is *Ecclesia*, the Church. Why then was she *presbytera*, elderly? Because she was created first of all things, and for her sake the world was framed (4. 1). The thought of the place in creation thus assigned to the Church necessitates a like broad conception of the relation of the Gospel to the universe. In this vision the Church hands her booklet to Hermas, bidding him return it to her when read (1. 3), for the revelation was not yet complete (4. 2).

In *Vis*. iii. she reappears with the six young men: says to them, Go and build: and shews Hermas the vision of a great tower being built by them upon the waters, of bright square stones, itself foursquare (2. 5). The tower (she tells him) is herself, the Church. It is the spiritual creation, which is established upon the floods (Ps. 24. 2), because your life was saved and shall be saved by water (1 Pet. 3. 20); and it is founded by the word of the almighty and glorious Name (3. 5), being the outcome of the preaching of the Gospel to the world. When she has done speaking, the six young men carry her away to the tower, and four others carry the bench thither (10. 1). The vision ends with an ostensible explanation of her three apparitions. In the first vision she was old and dying and seated on a chair, because every weak person sits on a chair that the weakness of his body may be comforted (11. 4). In the next she was standing, as if risen to new life, and was less aged than before (12. 1). In the third she looks quite young, but for her hair, and is very *joyous* and seated on a bench (10. 5). For as when to one sorrowing come *good tidings* he straightway forgetteth (Jas. 1. 24) the former sorrows, and giveth heed to naught but the tidings that he heard, and is strengthened thenceforth unto good, and his spirit is renewed through the joy which he received; so ye too have received renewal of your spirits by *seeing these good things*. And whereas thou sawest her seated on a *bench*, the position is a firm one; for the bench has *four feet* and stands firmly; for the world likewise is compacted of *four elements*. They then that have repented shall be completely young again and *founded* (Col. 1. 23), if they repented with their whole heart. Now thou hast the revelation complete. Thou shalt ask nothing more of revelation; but if aught be lacking yet it shall be revealed to thee (13. 2—4). Thus the vision ends.

A general view of the three visions confirms the hypothesis that the third alludes to the Gospel revelation as complete. *Vis.* i. described the Church under the old dispensation as decaying and old and ready to vanish away. She accordingly vanishes for the moment, and her chair is carried off and is not seen again. In *Vis.* iii. the bench takes its place; and at the end of the vision it is deposited in the tower, and thus becomes, as it should if it represents the Gospels, a permanent possession of the Church. The chair was her seat of teaching and authority under the former dispensation: what can her new seat the bench, which stands on four feet, signify but the fourfold Gospel? The word *founded*, from Col. 1. 23, is well chosen to express firm foundation on the faith of the Gospel by the word of the almighty and glorious Name. We may say then that it is the Four Gospels that are signified by the feet of the Church's seat, and that are likened to the four elements of the world.

The reader of the *Shepherd* will be struck by the

intricate connexion of its parts and the subtle way in which attention is called to this by the use of corresponding words and phrases.

Sim. ix. describes the building of the tower over again and at greater length than *Vis.* iii. The tower is, as we have seen, the spiritual counterpart of the creation, Hermas evidently following the same tradition as Papias and others, who interpreted the Mosaic cosmogony as a mystery of Christ and the Church. The tower in the similitude is built foursquare, so that it could contain the whole world (2. 1), and of stones from twelve mountains representing all the nations of the world (17. 1—2). But first of all four sets of stones come up out of the deep, and these make four *rows* or *tiers* in the foundation of the tower (4. 3). The word for rows being στοῖχοι, and the tower being a spiritual *cosmos*, the suspicion at once arises that the four rows are meant to correspond to the four στοιχεῖα or material elements spoken of in *Vis.* iii. 13, and to refer, like these, to the Four Gospels. To anglicise the wordplay we may say, that the elements of the foundation of the tower, in *Sim.* ix., correspond to the elements of the world. The words *I was joyous beholding such good things* (10. 1) are parallel to the words in *Vis.* iii. 13, *joyous* and *seeing these good things*, where the good things are the good tidings of the Gospel; and the expression *founded* in the vision answers to the setting of the four rows in the *foundation* of the tower. These links between the similitude and the vision confirm the suspicion that the fourfold foundation likewise adumbrates the fourfold Gospel.

But its four tiers are said, in the explanation of them given to Hermas, to mean the four generations or ages of the world from the beginning (15. 4); and what have pre-Christian generations to do with the Gospel of Christ? The answer is, that the Gospel, like the Church, is regarded by Hermas as ideally prior to the creation: that because the four tiers are parts of the tower or Church, the generations for which they stand must in some sense have been evangelized: and that the fourth and last generation, consisting of apostles and teachers of the preaching of the Son of God, is expressly said to have gone down to the underworld after death and preached to the preceding generations (16. 5). Each of the four so-called generations therefore had a Gospel preached to it, the generations being artificially reckoned so as to make the revelations to them correspond in number to the Canonical Gospels. The last revelation is curiously the actual Gospel delivered to the apostles, which includes the four Gospels. What Hermas hints at by his figures of the bench and the foundation of the tower is put into words by Irenaeus in his great work, the *Five Books against Heresies*.

The numbers of the stones in the four rows are 10, 25, 35 and 40 respectively (4. 3), of which the decades are expressed in Greek by the initials of John, Cephas, Luke and Matthew. S. Peter was the traditional authority for S. Mark's Gospel. Two *fives* remain, according to the best text, and a meaning might be suggested for these also; but we must pass on to the sayings of Irenaeus.

2. *S. Irenaeus of Lyons.*

The famous sayings of S. Irenaeus on the number of the Gospels gave a meaning to the figure of the bench in *Vis.* iii. 13 of Hermas as soon as it was seen that the Gospel was the subject of the passage. Then the thought occurred to me, Did Irenaeus borrow the idea of his sayings wholly or in part from Hermas? It was possible, for Hermas wrote a generation before him. Was it not only possible but probable? Eusebius gives the answer, in a passage quoted by Bp Lightfoot at p. 45 of his volume above mentioned. Eusebius is speaking of Irenaeus as a witness to the New Testament. First he gives his testimony to the Gospels: he goes on to the Apocalypse: afterwards he says, And he has made mention too of the First Epistle of John, adducing very many testimonies out of it, and likewise also of the First Epistle of Peter. *And he not only knows, but even receives the writing of the Shepherd, saying, Well then spake the Scripture which says, First of all believe that God is one, even He that created all things.* Thus we learn that Irenaeus received the *Shepherd* and quoted its first commandment as Scripture, which implies a very high degree of respect for the work. It was likely then or not unlikely that he would reproduce the ideas of Hermas on the Gospels, if they were sufficiently remarkable; and that they certainly were, if we are right in our interpretation of the hieroglyphs by which we have supposed the *Shepherd* to allude to the number of the Gospels.

In Iren. III. 11. 11—12 (ed. Harvey) we read, that there are not more than four Gospels, nor could there be fewer. For since there are four regions of the world, and four catholic winds, it was natural that the Church, which is spread over the whole earth, and has the Gospel for its *pillar* and stay and breath of life, should have *four pillars*, blowing incorruption from all quarters and rekindling mankind. The Word, the artificer of all things, that sits upon the Cherubim and holds the universe together, when He was manifested to men gave us the Gospel in four forms but held together by one Spirit. For the Cherubim are fourfaced (Ezek. 1. 6) and their faces are emblems of the working of the Son of God. For the living creatures have respectively the aspects of lion, calf, man, eagle. And the Gospels are consonant with these, upon which Christ sits. The Gospels of S. John, S. Luke, S. Matthew and S. Mark are then made to correspond to the living creatures in the above order, being characterised from their beginnings as (so to say) the *divine, priestly, human* and *spiritual* Gospels respectively. Correspondingly, continues Irenaeus, the Word conversed with the patriarchs as Divine: gave priestly ordinances to those under the Law: afterwards was made Man: and sent forth the gift of the Spirit to all the earth. This sending forth corresponds to S. Mark's, *Go ye into all the world...And they went forth and preached everywhere.* As was the working of the Son of God, which was quadriform, such was the form of the living creatures, and such the character of the Gospel. And on this account there were four catholic covenants given to humanity;

through Adam, Noah, Moses and our Lord Jesus Christ, according to the Latin version, or through Noah, Abraham, Moses and Christ, according to the Greek text of Irenaeus. The Gospels in some order correspond to these, the last in order corresponding to the actual Gospel covenant.

Hence they are idle and unlearned, nay and audacious, that deform the Gospel by wrongly admitting more or fewer than four faces of it. The Gospels of the Apostles only are true and firm, and it is impossible that there should be more or fewer than these, as we have shewn at such length. *For when God has made all things compounded and fitted together, the form of the Gospel too must needs have been well compounded and compacted.* This argument evidently assumes that the world is compacted *of four elements**.

The phrase "Gospels of the Apostles" illustrates Justin Martyr's *Memoirs of the Apostles*, and it is explained by the traditional ascription of the Four Gospels to the Apostles Matthew, Peter, Paul and John respectively. It remains to compare the series of sayings quoted from Irenaeus with the corresponding representations of Hermas.

---

* Διὰ τεσσάρων στοιχείων κρατεῖται (*Vis.* iii. 13): Tatian made a Gospel compounded of the Four Gospels, and called it the *Diatessaron*.

Hermas in *Vis.* iii. depicts the Church as seated on a bench with four feet, which represent the Four Gospels; and in *Sim.* ix. 1. 1 the Shepherd explains to him that the holy Spirit that had appeared to him in the form of the Church was the Son of God. Irenaeus says that the Son of God sits upon the four Cherubim, or living creatures, and that these correspond to the Four Gospels. Thus, briefly, both writers represent Christ as seated on the Four Gospels. With the Cherubim compare in Hermas the four young men who carry off the bench to the tower.

Hermas in *Vis.* iii. argues that the Gospels, the supports of the Church's seat, are four in number because the world is compacted of four elements. Irenaeus likewise concludes that the Gospel must have had four constituents, in order to correspond to the fabric of the universe, which was understood to be made up of four elements.

Hermas in *Sim.* ix. hints at the Four Gospels by the four rows in the foundation of the tower*: Irenaeus

* A study of the style of Hermas having led me to expect that his four στοιχεῖα would reappear somewhere in some disguise, the allusion to them in the four στοῖχοι seemed too obvious to be accidental. At first the writer seemed to say that the στοῖχοι had no connexion with the Gospels. But afterwards it was seen that he was merely giving their interpretation in two instalments: first, they were the four cosmic generations from the beginning (15. 4): next, they had had the Gospel

makes the Gospels the four pillars of the Church. Thus, briefly, both describe the Church as an edifice supported by the Four Gospels; and at the same time they liken them again implicitly to the four elements, the Church being conceived of as spread over, or able to contain the whole world.

The four rows in Hermas stand for cosmic generations, each of which had received a Gospel message corresponding to one of the Four Gospels. So, according to Irenaeus, the Logos revealed Himself to all the four generations, and each of them received a covenant, each revelation and covenant corresponding to one of the Canonical Gospels. The last generation in each case receives the actual Gospel, which comprises the Four Gospels. The Church in Irenaeus was the Gospel for its one pillar, and the Gospels for its four pillars: analogous to this in Hermas are the figures of the one bench with four feet and the one foundation with its four rows or tiers, representing the Gospel and the Gospels.

So many agreements of two writers in ideas so extraordinary cannot be accidental. Their obvious

preached to them (16. 5), and it was this that qualified them to be *four rows in the foundation of the tower* (4. 3), which was therefore (in a sense) founded upon the fourfold Gospel.

explanation is that Irenaeus borrowed more or less from Hermas, whose work, as Eusebius tells us, he not only knew but even received and quoted as Scripture. If it should ever be proved that there was some source from which the two may have drawn all that they had to say independently, this must have been of not later date than Hermas, and my case would not be impaired. I maintain on the strength of the evidence adduced, that the famous sayings of Irenaeus on the actual and necessary fourfoldness of the Gospel were not his own, but a reproduction of what Hermas had written a generation before: that Hermas, in his enigmatic way, represented the Four Gospels as having already obtained a unique and Canonical position: and that, in any case, they had obtained this position in the lifetime and to the knowledge of Hermas, who wrote, not in any obscure corner of the world, but in its capital, Rome.

3. *Pythagoras and Philo.*

The notion of Hermas and Irenaeus that the Four Gospels correspond to the four elements of the world implies that the Four Gospels were actually recognised by the Church when they wrote: that in the nature of things, according to their view of it, there could not have been more or fewer than Four Gospels: and that the Gospel as a unit corresponds to the world. This analysis makes it at once obvious that the notion was a development and had a history, and was not altogether and exclusively the product of one mind or one age.

In Iren. III. 11. 11 it was said that the Gospel corresponds to the working of the Logos, who holds all things together. That the Logos holds all things together (Wisd. I. 7) was a well-known doctrine of Philo, which was made use of even by New Testament writers. See Col. I. 17, with the illustrations in Bp Lightfoot's edition. From the Logos of Philo it was easy and natural for a Christian writer to pass to Christ, or the Church, or the Gospel; and when this had been brought into relation with the universe, it was no less natural, as soon as the Four Gospels had asserted their exclusive position, to compare them to the four elements of the world, making out that its constitution determined what must be the number of the Gospels. An interesting variation on the idea of Philo is found in chap. 6 of the *Epistle to Diognetus*, which teaches that, as the soul is in the body, so are Christians in the world. The soul is shut up in the body, but itself holds it together: and Christians are confined in the world as in prison, while it is they that hold the world together. According to the Midrash, Adam was created of cosmic dimensions, and his dust was taken from all parts of the earth. The *Sibylline Oracles* make his name an acrostic of the four points of the compass, NWES.

But the thought of the necessary fourfoldness of the Gospels was in part due to the Pythagoreans' doctrine of numbers, and especially to their theory of the *tetractys* or quaternion, the sum of the first four numbers. Irenaeus, in the first paragraph of his first Book, refers to the famous Pythagoric *tetractys* as the reputed root of all things.

Philo speaks in this way of the simple *tetrad* or number four, which he declares in *De Op. Mundi* 16 to have been the beginning or germ out of which all heaven and the world were evolved.

Hermas lets us know that he was acquainted with these speculations in cosmogony when he dwells upon the squareness of his cosmic tower and the several stones thereof. It was *similimembrius* (Iren. II. 15. 3), each part being like the whole. The rudimentary fact that square-faced figures fit well together and fill up space would have led the philosophers to imagine a primeval tetrad of which the world was symmetrically built up. Of kindred origin must have been the expression in Aristotle's *Eth. Nic.* I. 10. 11 for the perfect character, "foursquare without reproach."

To conclude, as soon as it was recognised that the "everlasting Gospel" was inherent in the system of things, and that the true "Gospels of the Apostles" were just four in number; these would be made out to be a manifestation of the mystic tetrad, and thus we should have come by a natural process of thought, and must sooner or later have come, to the at first sight strange comparison, as in Irenaeus and Hermas, of the Four Gospels to the Four Elements of the World. The reasoning of both writers alike may fail to satisfy; but beneath their *Argumentatio mere inepta* lies the solid fact, that the Church in their day was established on the same Four Gospels on which it still stands.

II.

HERMAS

AND

THE SYNOPTIC GOSPELS.

HERMAS AND THE SYNOPTIC GOSPELS.

The *Shepherd of Hermas* having been found to allude to the Canonical Gospels as four in number, it remains to shew that it makes free use of their subject matter and phraseology, although it never cites them expressly. But we shall first give some indication of the peculiar method of Hermas by an example of its application to the Old Testament followed by some illustrations from one of his favourite authorities, the Epistle of S. James.

In *Sim.* ix. we read, And he took me away to Arcadia, unto a certain rounded mountain, and set me on the top of the mountain; and he shewed me a great plain, and round about the plain twelve mountains (1. 4). And in the midst of the plain he shewed me a great white rock rising up out of the plain: the rock was higher than the mountains, foursquare, so that it could contain the whole world (2. 1). On the rock, above a gate hewn out of it, a tower is built of stones brought from all the mountains (4. 2, 5), in the last days (12. 3). The tower is the Church (13. 1). The rock on which it is built is therefore the mountain of the Lord's house; and its being higher than the mountains alludes to the saying of Micah 4. 1 and Isaiah 2. 2, *And it shall come to pass in the last days, that the mountain of the Lord's house shall be established in the top of the mountains, and shall be exalted above the hills; and all nations shall flow into it.* The twelve mountains, from which stones are brought for the building of the tower, represent all the nations of the world. This is a good example of allusion to a writing by or with the help of symbols, a method which Hermas applies with characteristic ingenuity in all parts of his work. We shall next give a few examples out of many of the use which he makes of the Epistle of S. James.

S. James i. 6 *But let him ask in faith, nothing wavering. For he that wavereth is like a wave of the sea driven with the wind and tossed. 7 For let not that man think that he shall receive anything of the Lord. 8 A doubleminded man is unstable in all his ways.* iv. 8 *Cleanse your hands, ye sinners; and purify your hearts, ye doubleminded.*

The word *doubleminded* and words related to it are much used by Hermas, and sometimes in contexts which point distinctly to S. James. Thus in *Mand.* ix. we read, For every *doubleminded man*, except he repent, shall hardly be saved: *cleanse* therefore *thy heart* from *doublemindedness;* and put on *faith*, for it is strong; and believe in God, that *thou shalt receive* all the things that thou *askest* (6—7). The epithet *unstable* or "unruly" (Jas. 3. 8) is attached to the demon of evil speaking (Jas. 4. 11) in *Mand.* ii. 3: in *Mand.* v. Hermas writes, And thenceforth, being filled with the evil spirits, he *is-unstable in all his* action, being drawn about hither and thither by the evil *spirits* (2. 7), these taking the place of the wind or winds in Jas. 1. 6: and in *Sim.* vi. he adds, For many who *are -unstable in their* plans project many things, and nothing succeeds at all with them; and they say that they are not helped-on-the-*way* in their actions, and... they *blame the Lord* (3. 5), as it is said in Jas. 1. 13, "I am tempted of God."

S. James i. 27 *Pure religion and undefiled before God and the Father is this, To visit the fatherless and widows in their affliction, and to keep himself unspotted from the world.*

Traces of this verse are found in *Mand.* ii. 7, And

thy heart *pure and undefiled: Vis.* iii. 9. 2, And *visit one another, and help one another: Mand.* viii. 10, To minister to *widows, to visit orphans* and those in want: *Sim.* i. 8, *Visit widows and orphans,* and overlook them not: *Vis.* iv. 3. 4, The gold part (on the head of the dragon) are ye that have escaped this *world*...5 [from which] they shall be *unspotted and pure* that are elect of God unto eternal life : *Sim.* v. 6. 7, For all flesh found *undefiled and unspotted,* in which the Holy Spirit dwelt, shall receive a reward. 7. 1...thy flesh *pure and undefiled*: *Sim.* ix. 26. 2, The stones that have the *spots* are dishonest deacons, who embezzled the livelihood of *widows and orphans,* and made gain of their ministry. Thus the verse is taken to pieces, and its parts are scattered all over the *Shepherd*.

S. James iv. 7 *Resist the devil, and he will flee from you.* 8 *Cleanse your hands, ye sinners &c.* 9 *Be afflicted, and mourn, and weep: let your laughter be turned to mourning, and your joy to heaviness.*

The use of verse 7 is very evident in *Mand.* xii., and attention is called to this by commentators. We have already shewn traces of verse 8 in the *Shepherd;* and the Church addresses Hermas in terms of verse 9 in *Vis.* i. 2. 2 sq., " Hermas, hail: and I, sorrowing and *weeping,* said, Lady, hail: and she said to me, Why art thou sullen, Hermas, the longsuffering and easy tempered, that wast *always laughing?* Why thus *heavy* (κατηφής) of aspect, and not joyous?" This well illustrates the light touch with which the author of the *Shepherd* handles his materials. As he deals with the Epistle of S. James and with the Old Testament, so he deals with other writings *; and among them, as it seems, the Four Gospels, with which we shall endeavour to shew that he was well acquainted, beginning with the Synoptic Gospels.

1. *The Nativity.*

Of the stones approved for the building of the tower some were shaped naturally and had no need to be hewn. Irenaeus suggests a meaning for this, which is found to fit in with the representations of Hermas. In Iren. III. 27 the prophet Daniel's *stone cut out without hands* is said to have prefigured Christ as to be

---

* A comparison of the *Shepherd* with the *Teaching* in the *Journal of Philology* led me to write thus of Hermas (XVIII. 324): *Of greater importance than the proof that Hermas knew the Didaché is the discovery of his way of using his authorities. He allegorises, he disintegrates, he amalgamates. He plays upon the sense or varies the form of a saying, he repeats its words in fresh combinations or replaces them by synonyms, but he will not cite a passage simply and in its entirety. This must be taken into account in estimating the value of the Shepherd as a witness to the canonical Books of the New Testament.*

born of a virgin. He was to come into the world as a stone from the earth by an act of God, without operation of the hands of *the men that hew stones*. Accordingly Isaiah wrote, "Therefore thus saith the Lord God, Behold, *I lay* in Zion *for a foundation* a stone, a tried stone, a precious corner stone." For His advent was to be not of the will of man, but of the will of God (Joh. i. 13). Irenaeus (III. 30) compares the framing of Adam by the hand of God, of unwrought or virgin earth. Hermas distinguishes between hewn and unhewn stones in both of his accounts of the building of the tower. Hewn stone might not be used for an altar of God (Ex. 20. 25).

In *Vis.* iii. the unhewn stones, which go of themselves into the building, signify those whom the Lord approved because they *walked in the straightness of the Lord* and directed themselves by His commandments (5. 3). S. Clement of Alexandria in *Paed.* I. 9 says that the iota of the name Iesus represents the straight and natural way; having in mind doubtless the familiar representation of the two ways by the letter Y, which was attributed to Pythagoras. Such play upon the forms of the letters would have been well understood in the days of Hermas, so that an allusion to Iesus in the words "walked in the *straightness* of the Lord" would have occasioned no difficulty. If such allusion there be, Hermas means the unhewn stones collectively to signify Christ, whom Irenaeus saw prefigured in Daniel by the stone cut out without hands. S. Clement near the end of *Strom.* VI. 16 further teaches that the *Decalogue* points to Iesus as the *Word*, the letter iota being the Greek figure for *Ten*.

In *Sim.* ix. ten square, bright, unhewn stones come up first from the deep, and twelve virgins together bear them stone by stone, and deliver them to the builders (3. 4). The virgins encircle the gate (4. 1), which is the Son of God incarnate (12. 3). The tower is built upon the rock, which is the Son of God, regarded as preexistent (12. 2): the *ten* stones completely cover the rock, and they make a foundation for the tower (4. 2): thus they represent the Son of God, who is Himself the foundation (14. 6), and we may suppose their number to refer again to the name Iesus. The stones brought from the twelve mountains are *hewn by the men*—"the men that hew stones" (Iren.), before they are carried through the gate by the virgins (4. 5); but the four rows of foundation stones, which come up from the deep (4. 3), are fitted and built into the tower unhewn, as being endued with singular native purity (16. 7). Thus the whole foundation, Christ, is of unhewn stone; so that in accordance with the symbolism of Iren. III. 27, He is immaculate and born of a virgin. We shall see that the twelve virgins represent the Holy Ghost.

2. *John the Baptist.*

The features of the Baptist may be traced in the Shepherd, the *angel of repentance* (*Sim.* ix. 1), and in his double the Shepherd, the angel of retribution (*Sim.* vi. 3). The title of the former, who is *sent* to dwell with Hermas (*Vis.* v.), is suggested by S. Mark I. 2, 4, "Behold, *I send my angel*...[to be a preacher] *of repentance.*" The Baptist wore a girdle of *a skin*, and did eat *locusts* and *wild honey*: men were in doubt who he was, and said, "Who art thou?" (Joh. 1. 19), and so Hermas says to the angel of repentance in *Vis.* v. 3, *Who art thou?* The severity of the angel of retribution answers to the preaching of the Baptist in Matt. 3. 7 sq., "O generation of vipers...bring forth fruit *worthy of repentance*...God is able of these *stones* to raise up children unto Abraham. And now also the ax is laid unto the root of the trees: therefore every tree which bringeth not forth good fruit is hewn down, and *cast into the fire.*" With this compare also in *Sim.* viii., For the Lord, being moved with compassion, sent me to give *repentance* to all, although some were not *worthy* on account of their deeds (11. 1). The worthy are those whose rods, cut from the great willow, are given back green and flourishing: their rods bring forth fruit which marks them as *worthy of repentance*. The building of the tower is a sustained illustration of the words, *God is able of these stones &c.* In *Sim.* iv. 4 the dry trees are cast into the fire. The two angels are clad in *skins* of the goat, corresponding to the Baptist's girdle of skin. Is there any sort of trace of the preacher's diet of *locusts* and *wild honey* in the *Shepherd*?

Before pronouncing that there is not, we must notice that Hermas has a way of going off at a word, and using it without too strict regard to the context from which he borrowed it. Thus, whereas in chap. 13 of the *Teaching*, it is said, "*When thou openest a jar of wine or oil*, take the firstfruits and give to the *prophets*;" Hermas, who has more to say against the false prophets than in favour of the true, takes occasion to make a parable of an empty jar packed away with jars of wine or oil, and to compare the false prophet to the empty jar (*Mand.* xi. 15). In *Mand.* v. he has a parable of a jar of *honey* made bitter by a little wormwood (1. 5), which may or may not have been suggested by the Baptist's "wild honey." The epithet of this honey is transferred to the angel of retribution, who is said in *Sim.* vi. to be as it were *wild* of aspect (2. 5), and bitter to the sheep (3. 2); and the locusts in the Gospel might easily have been transformed by two steps into the "fiery locusts" coming out of the mouth of the dragon in *Vis.* iv. 1. 6. These indeed may have been suggested by Rev. 9. 3 sq.; but if there had been no second mention of locusts in the New Testament, Hermas would have found material for a parable in S. John the Baptist's locust-food as he does in other kinds of food.

According to S. Luke 3. 21—22, Jesus being baptized by John, "and praying, the heaven was opened, And the Holy Ghost descended in a bodily shape." In *Vis.* i. 1. 4, Hermas "praying, the heaven was opened;" and in *Vis.* iii. and *Sim.* ix., as we shall see, the Spirit is represented in the bodily shape of seven women and twelve virgins respectively. The title "beloved son" (Luke 3. 22) is used in *Sim.* v. of the son of the owner of the field (2. 6), and it is said of him the son is the Holy Spirit (5. 2).

3. *The Temptation.*

Matt. 4. 1—11. Jesus was led up of the Spirit into the wilderness to be tempted of the devil. He fasts forty days, and the tempter comes to Him and says, If thou be the Son of God, command that these stones be made bread. He replies, *Man shall not live by bread alone, but by every word that proceedeth out of the mouth of God.* A mysterious episode is described in *Sim.* ix. 11, the full interpretation of which cannot be entered upon here. Hermas and the twelve virgins keep vigil by the tower, in preparation for a great revelation. They pray without ceasing, and in the morning the Shepherd comes and asks Hermas, On what didst thou sup? *I supped, Sir,* said he, *on words of the Lord all the night.* This fast, during which he was fed on *words of the Lord,* must have been suggested by the Gospel narrative of the Temptation.

Next, the devil takes Jesus to the holy city, sets Him on the pinnacle of the temple and says, If thou be the Son of God, cast thyself down: for it is written, He shall give His angels charge concerning thee : and *in their hands they shall bear thee up,* lest haply thou dash thy foot against a stone. Accordingly in *Vis.* i. 4 two so-called men "bear up" the Church, which adumbrates Christ, in their arms, and carry her off; and in *Vis.* iii. 10 the six young men carry her away to the tower. These men correspond also to the ministering angels of Matt. 4. 11. Temptation by the devil is spoken of in the *Shepherd* in *Mand.* xii. 5 and elsewhere. He prevails against the "empty;" but against the "full in the faith" he has no power, or gains but transient successes (*Sim.* ix. 31).

Lastly, the devil taketh Him unto an exceeding high mountain, *and sheweth Him all the kingdoms of the world, and the glory of them.* The physical impossibility of seeing all the kingdoms of the world from one spot has led to much speculation about this verse. The idea of it being so striking, Hermas would naturally have brought it into his allegory if he saw his way to do so. Now in *Sim.* ix. 1 (p. 25) the Shepherd takes Hermas to an Arcadian mountain top, and shews him a great plain surrounded by twe've mountains, which represent all the nations of the world. Thus, with his usual ingenuity, the writer brings in a clear though unobtrusive allusion to the scene of the third and last temptation, according to S. Matthew's reckoning.

4. *The Transfiguration.*

In *Sim.* ix. it is said of the gate cut out of the rock, The gate so *glistered* (ἔστιλβεν) above the sun that I marvelled at the brightness of the gate (2. 2). The gate meaning the Son of God, and the word for *glister* being found once only in the New Testament, namely in S. Mark's account of the Transfiguration, we may infer that Hermas borrowed the word from Mark 9. 3, "*And his garments became glistering* (R. V.), exceeding white; so as no fuller on earth can whiten them."

5. *The keys of the kingdom of heaven.*

It is said in Matt. 16. 18—19, "*Thou art Peter, and upon this rock I will build my church;* and the gates of hell shall not prevail against it. And I will give unto thee *the keys of the kingdom of heaven.*" The famous controversy on the meaning of the rock in verse 18 is of long standing. Hermas in *Sim.* ix. settles it for himself by making Christ the rock on which the tower or Church is built. The twelve virgins are the appointed guardians of the tower, and are ordered not to depart from it (5. 1). They stand round the gate (3. 2), and it is their function to carry all the stones for the building of the tower through the gate and deliver them to the builders, and any stones put into the building by the men, and not carried through the gate by the hands of the virgins are *unable to change their colours* and become fit for insertion in the tower (4. 6—8). The power of the keys therefore is in the hands of the virgins. What then do they represent? Assuming without proof for the present that they represent the Holy Spirit, we see at once from their number that they are the Holy Spirit as distributed to the Twelve Apostles. To these, in a sense, or strictly speaking to the Holy Spirit dwelling in them, Hermas represents the "keys of the kingdom of heaven" as given. They have the power to open and shut, and none can be admitted into the tower without having been passed by them through the gate. The change of the various colours of the stones approved, namely to white, is explained by Isaiah 1. 18, *Though your sins be as scarlet, they shall be white as snow; though they be red like crimson, they shall be as wool.* Those not brought through the gate by the virgins cannot obtain remission of sins, for it is said in the Fourth Gospel, "Receive ye the Holy Ghost: whose soever sins ye remit, they are remitted unto them; and whose soever sins ye retain, they are retained" (20. 22—24). This passage is referred to in *Sim.* ix. 25, where the apostles and teachers of the Gospel are said to have received the Holy Ghost.

6. *The Sower and other Parables.*

In chap. 9 of the *Teaching* is the striking Eucharistic prayer, "As this broken bread was once scattered in grains upon the mountains, and being gathered together became one; so let thy Church be gathered together from the ends of the earth unto thy kingdom. For thine is the glory and the power through Jesus Christ for ever." The idea of this is found in *Sim.* ix. of Hermas, but for bread he gives us a stone. Stones scattered upon the twelve mountains, which represent all the nations of the world, are brought together for the building of the tower; and this when it is finished shews no join, but looks like a single stone cut out of the rock, so completely do its many once scattered stones become one (9. 7). He deals in like manner with the parable of the Sower, replacing seeds again by stones.

In the Gospel parable there are three cases of failure and three degrees of success, the seed which falls on the good ground bringing forth thirty, sixty or a hundred-fold. In *Vis.* iii. 2. 9 some of the rejected stones, being thrown to a distance from the tower, fall on to the way, but roll aside to where there is no way, thus corresponding to the seeds which *fell by the way side:* other stones fall into the fire and are burned, corresponding to the seeds which, when the sun was up, *were scorched:* other stones fall near the waters and desire to roll into them, but are not able, thus corresponding to that which withered away because it *lacked moisture**. It is a feature of the parable of the Sower that an explanation of it is given, not without some censure of the disciples who require it. So the Church explains the parable of the stones to Hermas, at the same time reproving him for his curiosity in desiring to know all about the tower (3. 1). In the course of her exposition we come upon extracts from the Sower, such as *These are they that heard the word* (7. 3), and "*when affliction ariseth*, on account of their wealth and their affairs they utterly deny their Lord" (6. 5). The three cases of success in the Gospel parable have their counterparts in the three kinds

---

* Here the seed which fell upon stony ground is referred to twice, and that which fell among thorns is passed over. But this is referred to (as we shall see) in *Sim.* ix. 20.

of stones approved for the building of the tower; whereof the choicest are the foundation stones, and the remainder are distinguished in *Sim.* ix. as facing-stones and smaller stones which, like rubble, have to be placed on the inside (7. 5).

In *Sim.* ix. it is written, And from the third mountain, that had *thorns* and thistles, they that believed are such as these: some are wealthy, and some entangled in much business. The thistles are the rich, and the thorns they that are entangled in manifold business. These cleave not to the servants of God, but go astray and are *choked* by their transactions. And the rich hardly (δυσκόλως) cleave unto the servants of God, fearing lest they should be asked for something by them. Such therefore *shall hardly enter into the kingdom of God* (20. 1—2). The symbolism of the *thorns* and the being *choked* by the cares of business come from the parable of the Sower (Matt. 13. 22). The saying that the rich *shall hardly enter into the kingdom of God* points to a different context in the Gospels, where it is connected with the command to *sell that thou hast and give to the poor*, and with the saying, *It is easier for a camel to go through the eye of a needle than for a rich man to enter into the kingdom of God* (Matt. 19. 24). We may say then that

Hermas must have had his attention drawn to this, and that, the saying being so remarkable, he was likely to have made such use as he could of it. Now in *Vis.* iii. many stones lie round about the tower and not far from it, like the scribe who was *not far from the kingdom of God.* Some of them are *round,* humped stones which will not fit into their square places in the building (2. 8). Hermas asks what this signifies. How long will he be without understanding? The fine, round stones are they that have faith, but also worldly wealth, which, when affliction ariseth, leads men to deny their Lord. When will they be of use for the building? When their seductive wealth has been hewn away. For as the round stone, except some of its substance be cut off, cannot become square; so the rich in this world, except their wealth be cut away, cannot become fit for the Lord's use (6. 5—6). When they have been squared, they will fit into their places in the building; but how shall the condition of giving to the poor be satisfied? *Sim.* ix. explains this. The Lord orders their riches to be cut down, but not to be all taken away; so that they may be able to *do some good* with the residue and live unto God, seeing that they are of a goodly sort. Therefore they are cut round about a little and fitted into the tower (30. 5). They were hard to cut (6. 8), but the Lord of the tower so valued them [Mark 10. 21] that he would have some of them used (9. 4).

A few verses earlier in the Gospel is the saying, *Suffer the little children to come unto me, and forbid them not: for of such is the kingdom of God.* To this add the repeated saying that the *last shall be first*, and the words from the parable of the Vineyard, "beginning from the last unto the first" (Matt. 20. 8). Now in describing the twelve mountains in *Sim.* ix. 19—29, Hermas begins with the last in order of merit and ends with the first: "From the first mountain, the black one, they that believed are such as these: apostates and blasphemers against the Lord and betrayers of the servants of God...And from the twelfth mountain, the white one, they that believed are such as these: they are as babes into whose heart no guile entereth...As many of you, saith he, as shall continue and be as babes, not having guile, shall be more glorious than all the aforesaid. For all babes are glorious before God and *first* in His sight. Blessed then are ye, as many as put away wickedness from you and put on guilelessness: as *first* of all ye shall live unto God." Ye, the last, shall be first.

The parable of the Tares also is interpreted in

the Gospel, and it is said, *The field is the world:* so Hermas explains his parable of a Vineyard in *Sim.* v., and says, *The field is this world* (5. 2). Angels play a part in both parables. In the parable of Hermas it will be seen that expressions from several Gospel parables come in incidentally. In the parable of the Tares the wicked and the good look alike, and are only separated at the end of the world. Hermas changes tares to trees, as he changed seeds to stones, and gives us his own short parable in *Sim.* iii. of *many trees not having leaves*, which seem all alike dead in the winter of this world. *Sim.* iv. again is a parable of trees, *some sprouting and some dry:* the righteous shall dwell in the world to come, but the wicked shall be *burned* as logs, as it is said, bind the tares in bundles *to burn them* (Matt. 13. 30).

It would be in the manner of Hermas to turn the Mustard Seed into a hailstone. We may think therefore that his very small granule of hail in *Mand.* xi. 20 hints at that least of all seeds. Irenaeus in *Fragm.* 29 (quoted by Zahn) seems to connect *Sim.* viii., on the great willow overshadowing plains and mountains, with the mustard seed, and thus to suggest that Hermas was thinking of it again in his similitude. Those who give up their rods dry, but having a very little green (10. 3), are those who have faith as a grain of mustard seed, and repent and work righteousness. The reader of the *Shepherd* will easily find traces of other Gospel parables therein.

7. *Miracles and Signs.*

Most of the Gospel miracles were wrought upon the persons of men, the remainder being signs of lordship over the material world. The latter will be touched upon in the next section, on *Hermas and the Fourth Gospel*. Under the former head come miracles of healing, which the *Shepherd*, in the sections on the tower, converts into the shaping of stones rejected by the builders. Many such stones are seen in *Vis.* iii. *lying* about the tower, seamed, stunted, or otherwise unfit for use (2. 8); like the "great multitude of impotent folk, of blind, halt, withered," who *lay* about the pool of Bethesda, waiting to step or be *cast* into the water when it was troubled (Joh. 5. 7). In *Sim.* ix. the stones *lying* by the tower are given over to the Shepherd to cleanse, and he says that he will hew most of them, and *cast* them into the building (7. 1—4). Although *cleansing*, which goes with hewing (8. 4), applies to all the stones, it suggests in particular the cleansing of *lepers*, who are graphically symbolised by the stones with a scab or scurf (ἐψωριακότες). "These are they that denied and returned not unto their Lord, but became barren and desolate: they that cleave not to the servants of God, but keep apart and destroy their own souls" (26. 3). This is explained by the customary isolation of lepers and the spiritual death typified by their disease. Lastly, as it is said in the Gospels that some afflicted persons could not be healed, and that miracles in certain cases could not be wrought on account of men's hardness of heart and unbelief; so it is said in *Sim.* ix. that some of the stones were so hard that they could not be hewn (8. 6).

Akin to miracles of healing is the casting out of devils. The idea of possession by evil spirits runs through *Mand.* v. Men of little faith cannot cast out devils (Matt. 17. 20); but they that have much faith withstand the devil, and he departs from them, finding no entrance (*Mand.* xii. 5). Hermas personifies evil speaking and the like, and selfwill, as demons, in *Mand.* ii. 3 and *Sim.* ix. 22—23. He makes double-mindedness a daughter of the devil (*Mand.* ix. 9), grief and sharp temper her sisters (x. 1. 1), and evil desire a daughter of the devil (xii. 2. 2); somewhat as in the Gospel persons whose works are evil are called children of the devil. We need not now attempt to disentangle the writer's doctrine of demoniacal possession from its allegorical accessories: it is enough to see that he writes as such a writer might have written with the Gospels as his point of departure. A conspicuous word in these is δύναμις, in the sense both of divine *power* and of its manifestation by miracles or "mighty works." Hermas takes it up and uses it frequently: he calls one of his twelve virgins *Power*; and in *Mandates* vii. ix. xi. xii. he insists upon the lack of *power* in the devil and all that is earthly, and upon the *power* of faith and of the Holy Spirit, as coming "from above."

Of signs, the *Shepherd* seems to glance at the sign of the prophet Jonah, when in *Vis.* iv. 1 it compares the great beast which Hermas encounters to a κῆτος* (Matt. 12. 40), that is a "whale" or *sea-monster* (R. V. marg.). The comparison does not of itself help us much to determine the creature's form, since in a figurative work any sort of monster might be regarded as coming up out of the sea (Rev. 13. 1); but it does point, and may have been intended merely to point,

---

* The most effective word to describe the beast is *dragon*, which is an alternative to κῆτος in the Greek of Gen. 1. 21. The beast seems to be of a composite order, as we shall indicate in a subsequent section.

to the one place in the New Testament where the word "whale" occurs, and thus to the sign of Jonah.

8. *The cleansing of the Tower.*

In *Sim.* ix. 6—7 a great array of men are seen to approach, and among them one of such lofty stature as to overtop the tower. He scrutinises every stone of it, and strikes each with a rod three times. Some thereupon become black as "a coal" (Lam. 4. 8), and others are found faulty in one way or other. All these are cast out and laid by the side of the tower, and other stones are put in their place. The stones which had been laid aside are then ordered to be cleansed carefully: those which will fit in are replaced in the building: and the rest are cast far away from the tower. Searching the Gospels for parallels to the approach of the colossal man in his glory, to test and discriminate between the stones that had been placed in the walls of the tower, we notice in Matt. 25. 31 sq., *When the Son of man shall come in his glory, and all the holy angels with him, then shall he sit upon the throne of his glory: And before him shall be gathered all nations: and he shall separate them one from another, as a shepherd divideth his sheep from the goats &c.* This accounts for the attendant array of "men" or angels in the similitude. The process of testing may be described after the manner of the Baptist, with stones again for seeds, and with a phrase borrowed from *Sim.* ix. 30. 3, in the words, *His rod is in his hand, and he throughly purges his tower:* the charring of worthless stones at the touch of the rod represents the burning of the chaff in Matt. 3. 12. A further question might be asked, Are the Gospel narratives of the cleansing of the temple also hinted at by the cleansing of the tower?

9. *The Cross.*

It is a commonplace in patristic literature that the Crucifixion was prefigured by Isaiah 65. 2, "I have *spread out my hands* all the day unto a rebellious people;" and by the holding up of the hands of Moses by Aaron and Hur, whereby Jesus (Acts 7. 45) was enabled to discomfit Amalek at Rephidim (Ex. 17. 12). The *Teaching*, in its last chapter, enumerates three signs of the truth, the first the sign of an *outspreading* (ἐκπέτασις) in heaven. The meaning of this is disputed; but it seems to denote a spreading out as of bright clouds (Job 36. 29) in heaven, so as to form *a cross*. Interpreting the sign thus, I assumed that traces of it were to be found in Hermas; feeling that, whatever else might have led him to denote cruciform extension by mere extension not so defined, the fact that this "sign" was in the *Teaching* was good ground for the surmise that it was not absent from the *Shepherd*. And first I found a trace of it in *Vis.* iv., which will be commented upon under the head of *Hermas and the Fourth Gospel*. Next I noticed in *Sim.* ix., And the virgins *had spread out their hands*, as if about to receive something from the men (3. 2). Here was the phrase which in Isaiah was understood to point to the Crucifixion; in the *Shepherd* it clearly had a mystic meaning, for it is said that such stones as were not borne through the gate, the Son of God, by the hands of the virgins, could not change their colours (4. 8); and, the allusion in change of colours being obviously to the remission of sins (p. 38), a reference to the Cross* and the Atonement was seen to be appropriate and necessary. Thus the context justified the interpretation suggested by the *Teaching*.

In *Vis.* iii. 2 actual *crosses* are spoken of, and an indirect allusion to the Crucifixion follows. But first

---

* Remission of sins through the Holy Ghost presupposes the Crucifixion, as in Joh. 20. 20 sq. Accordingly the virgins, who represent the Holy Ghost, sign the stones with the sign of the Cross.

there is a display of courtesy between the Church and Hermas. She says to him, Sit thou here (Jas. 2. 3) upon the bench, and she insists upon his being seated while she stands, although he prays her to be seated first. But when he assays to seat himself upon the right hand, to his vexation she motions him to the left. He had been unmindful of the Lord's saying, "Sit not down in the highest room" (Luke 14. 8). The right hand was for those who had won a certain honour, as having suffered scourgings, imprisonments, great afflictions, *crosses*, wild beasts for the Name. When therefore she at last seats herself upon the right, she claims to have suffered *crosses*, as she has indeed done in the person of all her members who had undergone that form of martyrdom. But since the Church is also a manifestation of the Son of God, her session on the right hand implies in particular the Crucifixion of Christ, and His consequent exaltation to the right hand of God, according to S. Mark 16. 19, and Heb. 12. 2 and other passages.

10. *The final mission of the Apostles.*

S. Matthew's Gospel ends thus (28. 18—20), "All power is given unto me in heaven and in earth. Go ye therefore, and teach all nations, baptizing them in the name of the Father, and of the Son, and of the Holy Ghost. Teaching them to observe all things whatsoever I have commanded you: and lo, I am with you alway, even unto the end of the world. Amen." In S. Mark 16. 15—16 the apostles are commanded, *Go ye into all the world, and preach the Gospel to the whole creation. He that believeth and is baptized shall be saved.* According to S. John 20. 22, Jesus "breathed on them, and saith unto them, *Receive ye the Holy Ghost.*" These three passages seem to be referred to in *Sim.* ix. 25: "And from the eighth mountain, where were the many springs, and the whole creation of the Lord was watered by the springs, they that believed are of this sort: apostles and teachers who preached to all the world and who taught reverendly and purely the word of the Lord, and kept back nothing at all for evil desire, but always walked in righteousness and truth, as they also received the Holy Ghost." With *All power is given unto me &c.* (Matt. 28. 18), and with the saying, *that the Son of man hath power on earth to forgive sins,* (Matt. 9. 6), and other like passages, compare in *Mand.* iv., And concerning his former sin, there is one that can give healing; for He it is that hath the power over all things (1. 11). Unto me is given the power over this repentance (3. 5).

The commission to preach *to the whole creation* (Mark 16. 15), followed by the requirement of baptism, suggests an explanation of one of the most singular sections in the *Shepherd*, the account in *Sim.* ix. of the apostles' preaching to and baptizing the men of former ages from the beginning of the world. Why did the foundation stones of the tower come up from the deep, wearing the spirits of the virgins? Because they must needs have come up through water, that they might be made alive. The stones of the fourth row were the apostles and teachers who preached the Son of God. These, having fallen asleep in the power and faith of the Son of God, went down and preached also to them that had fallen asleep aforetime (προκεκοιμημένοις), and themselves gave them the seal of the preaching (16. 1—5). Hermas goes on to speak of the twelve mountains, representing the nations of *all the world*, to which the Son of God was *preached* (17. 1). Observing the reference in "preached to all the world," to S. Mark 16. 15, we may from the same verse account for the preachers' ministry in Hades as follows.

First there is a tacit allusion to the descent of

Christ to "the heart of the earth" (Matt. 12. 40), or Sheol, which is typified by the belly of the fish in Jonah 2. 2, and His preaching to the spirits in prison (1 Pet. 3. 19). After this S. Mark's form of the Lord's last words is a sufficient hint to Hermas to make the disciples do as He had done; and so, because they had to preach to the *whole creation*, and did accordingly preach *everywhere*, he makes them preach, not only upon earth, but in Sheol, and not only to living men, but to all the bygone generations from the beginning of the creation.

The notion of Hermas that Christ must have been preached to the four ages of the world may have suggested to Irenaeus (II. 33. 2) that He must have lived long enough upon earth to sanctify the four ages of man, by being an infant to infants, a child to children, a youth to youth, an elder to elders*. We find in Irenaeus the apocryphal citation, *The holy Lord remembered his dead who fell asleep aforetime* (IV. 55. 3), *and descended to them to preach the Gospel of his salvation, that he might save them* (III. 22. 1). This was known to Justin Martyr (*Trypho* 72), and

---

* This illustrates the principle that the Gospel as preached to the four generations or ages of the world must have had "four faces," each age desiderating a Gospel conformed to itself.

may have been known to Hermas. The very rare compound *fell-asleep-aforetime*, which is not found in Justin, may have been borrowed by Irenaeus (*praedormierunt*) from Hermas.

11. *The baptismal formula.*

The full baptismal formula (Matt. 28. 19) is not found in the *Shepherd*, but a special search reveals hidden traces of it therein. The short form from the Acts of the Apostles occurs in *Vis.* iii., These are they that heard the word, and were willing to be baptized into the name of the Lord (7. 3).

S. Luke 3. 22 suggests the representation of the Spirit "in a bodily shape." The Hebrew for spirit being feminine, the Spirit was sometimes represented as a woman. Hermas goes a step further, and resolves the one woman into seven women in *Vis.* iii., and into twelve virgins in *Sim.* ix. These by their plurality represent the distributions of the Holy Ghost (Heb. 2. 4); but their personalities are everywhere inseparable, and their oneness* and their significance are carefully indicated by the form of expression, "clad in the Holy Spirit of these virgins" (24. 2).

* Those clad in these spirits become one spirit (13. 5).

The virgins then represent the Holy Ghost. Now in *Sim.* ix. we read, that the tower is the Church, and that no man can be found in the kingdom of God, unless the virgins have clothed him with their *garment* (Matt. 22. 11); for if thou receive the Name only, and receive not the garment from these, it profiteth thee nothing. For these virgins are *powers of the Son of God*. The names themselves are their raiment. Whosoever wears the name of the Son of God should wear their names also; for *the Son himself wears the names of these virgins* (13. 1—3). To be baptized into Christ is to put on Christ (Gal. 3. 27). To be baptized into His name is to put it on and wear it as a garment: "They that *wear* soft raiment are in kings' houses" (Matt. 11. 8): "As we have *worn* the image of the earthy, we shall also *wear* the image of the heavenly" (1 Cor. 15. 49). He who would enter into the kingdom of heaven must be baptized into the name of the Son and into the name of the Holy Ghost; or, as Hermas expresses it, he must *wear the name of the Son of God and the names of the virgins*. The Son himself wears their names, for He was baptized, and the Spirit descended upon Him. But the virgins are also powers of the Son of God: that is to say, the Spirit proceeds from the Son. The identification of the twelve virgins with the Holy Ghost is confirmed by the way in which it works out in the various contexts which make mention of the virgins.

12. *The ending of S. Mark's Gospel.*

The last twelve verses of the Gospel according to S. Mark (16. 9—20) have been said to be no integral part of it; but to have been appended in more or less primitive times to the original or what remained of it, according as it was conjectured that the Evangelist's work was left unfinished, or that its last section was soon lost. The question has been debated at great length, and much learning has been brought to bear upon it. Here it would be out of place to do much more than seek for possible traces of the disputed section in the *Shepherd*, which we accordingly proceed to do, giving the verses themselves as rendered by the revisers of 1881.

9—11] *Now when he was risen early on the first day of the week, he appeared first to Mary Magdalene, from whom he had cast out seven devils. She went and told them that had been with him, as they mourned and wept. And they, when they heard that he was alive, and had been seen of her, disbelieved.*

12—13] *And after these things he was manifested in another form unto two of them, as they walked, on their way into the country. And they went away and told it unto the rest: neither believed they them.* The expression "manifested" is to be noticed, and the manner and the occasion of the manifestation. Hermas, as if imitating S. Mark, writes in *Sim.* ii. 1, *As I walked into the country*...the Shepherd *is manifested unto me*, and saith &c. In *Vis.* i. 1 and again in *Vis.* ii. 1 he is *walking* when the Spirit carries him away: in *Vis.* iii. 1 he is summoned *into the country* that the Church may appear to him: in *Vis.* iv. 1 he is *walking...into the country* when he encounters the great beast. The idea of change of form is illustrated by the different forms of the Church. In *Vis.* v. 4 Hermas fails to recognise the Shepherd (Luke 24. 16), until his aspect is changed.

14] *And afterward he was manifested unto the eleven themselves as they sat at meat; and he upbraided them with their unbelief and hardness of heart, because they believed not them which had seen him after he was risen.* A salient feature of the section is its censure of unbelief (ἀπιστία), and its requirement of faith for salvation (ver. 16). All this is found in the *Shepherd*, where, not to speak of the repeated denunciation of doublemindedness, one of the opposites of faith (*Mand.* xi.), there is an express contrast of Faith and Unfaith (ἀπιστία); the former in *Sim.* ix. being the first of the twelve virgins, whose ways lead to the house of God (14. 1), and the latter the first of the twelve women in black, who slay their votaries (20. 4). Faith is also the first of the seven holy women who bear up the tower in *Vis.* iii., and *through her* the elect of God *are saved* (8. 3). The word *hardness of heart* is found in Matt. 19. 8 and Mark 10. 5; and is used in *Vis.* iii. 7. 6, "they are not saved because of their hardness of heart."

15—16] *And he said unto them, Go ye into all the world, and preach the Gospel to the whole creation. He that believeth and is baptized shall be saved; but he that disbelieveth shall be condemned.* Here only do we find the command to preach the Gospel to the whole creation: in Col. 1. 23 it is narrated that it was so preached. S. Mark in two places has the phrase *from the beginning of the creation*, and he alone of the Evangelists has the words *creation* and *create* (10. 6; 13. 19), which are used so frequently by Hermas. The building of the tower is an obvious allegory of the preaching of the Gospel of Christ; and if this was to be preached to all the world, it was natural (if not necessary) that the tower should be made able to contain "the whole world." A stronger expression is "the whole creation;" and Hermas, as we have seen, spiritualises the cosmogony, and identifies his tower with the creation (p. 7). He does this as nearly as may be in express terms, making the Church reply to Hermas in *Vis.* iii., that the builders of the tower were the first created holy angels, to whom the Lord delivered His whole creation, to increase, and to build, and to rule over the whole creation (4. 1). Thus the tower is built by the builders of the creation: its building is the effectual preaching of Christ: and therefore the command, *Go ye and edify* (1. 7), is the command in S. Mark 16. 15 to preach the Gospel to the whole creation: and the necessity of baptism (ver. 16) is symbolised in *Vis.* iii. by the foundation of the tower upon the waters (p. 7). We have seen that these verses explain why the preachers preached to the men of the past, as in *Sim.* ix. 16, and we have found another allusion to them in *Sim.* ix. 25, where the watering from the many springs is a symbol of the baptism of "the whole creation of the Lord" (p. 52). Add that in *Sim.* viii. the great willow is the law of God given to the whole world, which law is the Son of God preached to the ends of the earth, and given into the heart of believers (3. 2—3); and that the dry rods are baptized, in the hope that most of them may come to life again (2. 9).

17—18] *And these signs shall follow them that believe: in my name shall they cast out devils; they shall speak with new tongues; they shall take up serpents, and if they drink any deadly thing, it shall in no wise hurt them; they shall lay hands on the sick, and they shall recover.* That true believers can work wonders is a leading doctrine of the *Shepherd.* On account of his *faith* (2. 4) Hermas is not harmed at all by the beast in *Vis.* iv. He who believes is able to cast off all wickedness (*Mand.* i.), and drive away the devil (xii. 5. 4). Hermas, slightly varying the word for *deadly*, speaks in *Mand.* xii. of *deadly lusts*, daughters of the devil (2. 2—3); and in *Sim.* ix. of *deadly reptiles*, living on the *dry* mountain, that destroy men (1. 9). Poison, with him, is carried not in boxes, but in the heart (*Vis.* iii. 9); or means harmful words (*Sim.* ix. 26). Sin is a sickness, which will be healed if men believe (*Mand.* xii. 6. 2). Somewhat in this way he would have used the above verses, if he had known them and thought fit to use them.

19—20] *So then the Lord Jesus, after he had spoken unto them, was received up into heaven, and sat down at the right hand of God. And they went forth, and preached everywhere, the Lord working with them, and confirming the word by the signs that followed. Amen.* To be *received up* is a word used of the Ascension here, and in Acts 1, and in 1 Tim. 3. 16 only in the New Testament. Rhoda in *Vis.* i., looking down from heaven, says *I was received up &c.* (1. 5). When it is said in *Vis.* iii. that the Church seated herself upon the right hand (2. 4), this is a figurative rendering of the statement of S. Mark, which is unique in the Gospels, that "the Lord Jesus...sat down at the right hand of God." Seated at the right hand upon the bench, the fourfold Gospel, the Church raises a bright rod, and says, "Seest thou a great thing," the building of the tower? The idea of the rod is from Ps. 110, "Sit thou at my right hand...The Lord shall send forth the rod of thy strength." Thus in the *Shepherd* we see in a figure the Lord's session at the right hand of God, accompanied by a sign of the confirmation of the word; the universal preaching of which is symbolised by the building of a world-wide tower, whose base goes down to the roots of the creation. The waving of a wand is the natural precursor of a "sign," for which "great thing" is a synonym, as in Iren. III. 26. 2.

If we had known beforehand that Hermas knew the last twelve verses of S. Mark, we should not have expected him to use them more largely; for, not to speak of turns of expression which they may have suggested to him, they underlie his parables of the Great Willow and the Tower. The inference from the *Shepherd* itself that he knew them is confirmed by the comparison of other writings, as below.

In searching for signs of acquaintance with the Gospels in early Church writers, we must make allowance for their tendency to express the New Testament in terms of the Old. Thus in *Epist. Barn.* 11 we read, "Let us enquire whether the Lord was minded to manifest beforehand concerning the Water and the Cross. Concerning the water it is written of Israel how that they would not receive the baptism that brings remission of sins, but would build for themselves. For the prophet saith (Jer. 2. 13)... *they abandoned me the spring of life, and they digged for themselves a pit of death*... And again he saith in another prophet (Ps. 1. 3 sq.), *And he that doeth these things shall be as the tree that is planted at the partings of the waters &c.*" From the bare mention of the

Cross and Baptism we gather that Barnabas had knowledge of some sort of written or oral Gospel; but he tells us little or nothing of its form, his one anxiety being to make out that the substance of it was manifested beforehand in the Prophets and the Psalms. He finds the Water and the Cross again in the *river* and the *trees* of Ezek. 47. 1—12, ending his quotation with a seeming reminiscence of S. John 6. 51, *And whosoever shall eat of them shall live for ever.* In like manner Irenaeus, who cites Mark 16. 19 as S. Mark's, interweaves allusions to the Old and New Testaments as follows (III. 11. 6), "Wherefore also Mark, the interpreter and follower of Peter, begins his Gospel thus, *The beginning of the Gospel of Jesus Christ, the Son of God, as it is written in the prophets, Behold I send my messenger before thy face, who shall prepare thy way. The voice of one crying in the desert, Prepare ye the way of the Lord: make straight paths before our God* (Mark 1. 1 sq.); manifestly saying that the voices of the holy prophets were the beginning of the Gospel, and pointing to Him whom they confessed to be Lord and God as the Father of our Lord Jesus Christ, who also promised to send him His angel before his face: which angel was John, crying in the spirit and power of Elias

(Luke 1. 17) in the wilderness, *Prepare ye the way of the Lord, make straight paths before our God...* Now at the end of his Gospel Mark sayeth, *So then the Lord Jesus, after he had spoken unto them, was received up into heaven, and sitteth at the right hand of God* (Mark 16. 19), confirming what was said [ver. 20] by the prophet (Ps. 110. 1), *The Lord said unto my Lord, Sit thou at my right hand, until I make thy enemies thy footstool.*" Thus Irenaeus not only quotes the received ending of S. Mark's Gospel, but declares it to be entirely consonant with the beginning. In another place (IV. 56. 3—4) he alludes cursorily to the words, *And they went forth and preached everywhere* (Mark 16. 20), thus: First he quotes Isaiah 2. 3—4, *For from Sion shall go forth a law, and the word of the Lord from Jerusalem &c.* Then he continues, "Now if the law of liberty, that is *the word of God proclaimed to all the earth by the Apostles, who went forth from Jerusalem,* had such effect as to change swords and spears into implements of peace...so that men now know not how to fight, but when smitten turn the other cheek (Matt. 5. 39); the prophets spake these things not of some other man (Acts 8. 34), but of our Lord who did these things." Thus he says that the apostles, in pursuance of their charge to preach to all the world, *went forth from Jerusalem* into all the earth; quoting *went forth* from S. Mark, and adding *from Jerusalem*, or Sion, from the Old Testament.

Justin Martyr refers in like fashion to the last verse of S. Mark, if not to other verses also of the disputed twelve, writing in *Apol.* 1. 45, "Now that God the Father of all would take the Christ to heaven after raising him from the dead, and keep him there until He should have smitten the demons hostile to him...hear the things said by David the prophet, which are these: *The Lord said unto my Lord, Sit thou at my right hand, until I make thy enemies thy footstool. A rod of power shall the Lord send forth for thee from Jerusalem*... thus making proclamation beforehand of the strong [Wisd. 18. 15] *word, which his apostles went forth from Jerusalem and preached everywhere.*" They "*went forth* and preached everywhere," he says, according to S. Mark; the words *from Jerusalem* being interpolated from the Old Testament, as we have seen that they were by Irenaeus. The expression "strong word" sufficiently alludes to the Lord's *confirming the word* (ver. 20); and the fact of the session at the right hand of God (ver. 19) is expressed in terms of one of the

Psalms of David. The Ascension is described as a taking (ἀγαγεῖν) to heaven, synonymously with S. Mark's *receive up;* and the mention of the subsequent smiting of the hostile demons, as if predicted in the Psalm quoted, is accounted for by S. Mark's *signs that followed* (ver. 20), whereof one was, *In my Name shall they cast out devils* (ver. 17). From Justin's words in themselves and in relation to words of Irenaeus we may infer that the earlier writer also was familiar with the peroration of S. Mark; and if Justin knew it, it would probably have been known to Hermas. That it was known to Hermas we have inferred from the phenomena of his own work; and the case for his reference to it in *Vis.* iii. 2. 4 (p. 62), partly in terms of the Old Testament, is strengthened by the fact and the manner of Justin's allusion to it in his first *Apology*, and especially by the correspondence of his Messianic rod of dominion with the bright rod waved by the Church, as she sits upon the bench and shews the sign of the building of the tower.

In chapter 15 of the *Apology of Aristides* it is said of the Lord Jesus Christ, *The fame of whose advent thou mayest know, O king, by reading their Evangelic Holy Scripture, as they call it. He had twelve disciples, who after his ascent to heaven went forth to the pro-*

vinces of the inhabited (world), and taught his majesty. Their written Gospel or Gospels must accordingly have narrated that the Lord *ascended* to heaven; that *He sat down at the right hand of God*, sharing the majesty on high (Heb. 1. 3); and that the disciples *went forth* and preached everywhere. These things are all recorded in S. Mark 16. 9—20, and two of them nowhere else in our Gospels. The same verses account for the addition to Acts 1. 2 in Codex Bezae, *And he commanded to preach the Gospel.*

The *Apology of Aristides* is edited by Prof. J. R. Harris and Mr J. A. Robinson in the first number of the Cambridge *Texts and Studies* (1891). The above citation from the *Apology* is from the Greek (p. 110), and it corresponds to words of chapter 2 in the Syriac (p. 36), and to the latter part of the little that is now extant of the Armenian (p. 30 sq.).

III.

HERMAS

AND

THE FOURTH GOSPEL.

HERMAS AND THE FOURTH GOSPEL.

In this section the chapters of the Fourth Gospel are taken in their order, and traces of them are sought in the *Shepherd of Hermas*.

Chap. i. 1 *In the beginning was the Word, and the Word was with God, and the Word was God.* 3 *All things were made by him; and without him was not anything made that was made.* 9 *That was the true Light, which lighteth every man that cometh into the world.* 12 *But as many as received him, to them gave he power to become children of God.* 13 *Which were born, not of...the will of man, but of God.* 14 *And the Word was made flesh, and dwelt among us.* 33 *Upon whom thou shalt see the Spirit descending, and remaining on him, the same is he.* 34 *And I saw, and bare record that this is the Son of God.* 51 *Hereafter ye shall see heaven open, and the angels of God ascending and descending upon the Son of man.*

1, 3, 14] The prologue of the Fourth Gospel enunciates the doctrine of the personal Logos or Word, who existed in the beginning, and was God: by whom all things were made: and who *became flesh*, and dwelt or *tabernacled* (ἐσκήνωσεν) among us. It might have been anticipated that the Christian teacher would sometimes vary the abstruse terminology of the doctrine, for the purpose of bringing it home to his less instructed hearers. The Logos, he would have said, means Christ: and then, working backwards from the phrase "became *flesh*," he could scarcely have avoided the antithesis, that He preexisted as *Spirit*. Taking now, for example, the homily called S. Clement of Rome's *Second Epistle to the Corinthians*, we read in its prologue, *Brethren, we ought so to think of Jesus Christ as of God*, corresponding to "the Word was God;" and a little below, For He graciously gave us *the light;* and in chap. 10, Let us flee ungodliness, lest evils *overtake us*, where there is perhaps a reminiscence of Joh. 1. 5 (cf. 12. 35...*lest darkness overtake you*). Chap. 9 of the homily runs thus, And let none of you say that this flesh is not judged, nor riseth again. Know ye, In what, but in this flesh, were ye saved? in what did ye recover sight? We ought therefore to guard the flesh as a temple of God. For like as ye were called in the flesh, in the flesh ye shall also come. If Christ the Lord, who saved us, *being first Spirit, became flesh*, and so called us, so *we also in this flesh shall receive the reward*. Let us therefore love one another &c. (1—5). The Word, "being" from the beginning as *Spirit*, became *flesh*. Singularly like Clem. Rom. II. 9 is the passage in *Sim.* v. of Hermas, *The pre-existent Holy Spirit, that created all the creation, did God make to dwell in flesh* which He chose...For the way of this flesh was well pleasing, because it defiled not itself upon earth, having the Holy Spirit. He took counsel therefore with the Son and the glorious angels, that this flesh also, having served the Spirit blamelessly, might have some place *of tabernacling* (κατασκηνώσεως), and might not seem to have lost the reward of its service. *For all flesh found undefiled and unspotted, wherein the Holy Spirit dwelt, shall receive a reward* (6. 5—7). Both writers seem to start from the Logos doctrine, and each varies its expression in his own way; the one copies the phrase *became flesh*, while the other alludes to the complementary clause *and tabernacled among us* (and at the same time to Ps. 16. 9 or Acts 2. 26) by means of the rare substantive rendered "nest" in Matt. 8. 20:

both pass from the flesh of Christ to flesh generally, in which the Spirit has dwelt, and its reward: Hermas adds words to the effect that by the preexistent Holy Spirit "all things were made" (Joh. 1. 3). The passage from the homily seems to have further affinities with the Fourth Gospel; and its phrases *come in the flesh* and *let us love one another* have the ring of the Epistles of S. John. If the homilist drew from the Johannine writings, this strengthens the case for the dependence of the *Shepherd* upon them.

Hermas in *Sim.* ix. 12 uses the rock, which was *old*, and the gate, which was *new*, as symbols of Christ preexistent and Christ incarnate respectively. How (asks Hermas) can both rock and gate represent the Son of God, if the one is old and the other new? Hermas is without understanding. The Son of God was begotten before the whole creation, and became the Father's counsellor in His creation: therefore, as symbolised by the rock, He is *old*. And why was the gate *new?* Because in the last days of the consummation He became *manifest* "in the flesh" (1 Tim. 3. 16). Therefore was the gate new, that such as were to be saved might enter through it into the kingdom of God (12. 1—3). A link between *Sim.* ix. 12 and the Gospel doctrine of the Logos is chap. 11 of the *Epistle to Diognetus*, which speaks expressly of the Word as He *which was from the beginning* (1 Joh. 1. 1), who appeared as *new* and was *old*. The writer of chapters 11—12, which do not properly belong to the *Epistle*, but have been run on to it by a clerical error, was probably acquainted with the *Shepherd of Hermas*, with which he agrees also in spiritualising the cosmogony, making them that love God a Paradise of Delight. It is somewhat strange to speak of Christ as new and old, in the sense of the *Epistle;* but it was natural in Hermas to identify the Son of God figuratively with a thing new and a thing old; and the later writer may have alluded briefly to this, transferring the epithets of the symbols to the Person signified. His use of these epithets, as descriptive of the Logos, confirms the impression that the same connexion of thought was in the mind of Hermas.

9] In the *glistering* of the gate we found a verbal allusion to the Transfiguration as described by S. Mark, who records that *His garments became glistering* (p. 37); but something more than this must be meant by the intense intrinsic brightness of the gate, which answers so well to the description of the Son of God as the "true Light," the preternatural light of men.

12—13] For *Which were born* there is an alternative reading *Which was born** (ver. 13), suiting the application of the verse by Irenaeus to the nativity of Christ (p. 30), while giving the sense, that *He who was born not of the will of man but of God* empowered believers on His Name to become children of God (ver. 12). Such, with either reading, they are said to become, and as such they are potentially like Him (1 Joh. 3. 2): as He is, so are we in this world (4. 17). He says, *I am the Light of the world* (Joh. 8. 12), and *Ye are the light of the world* (Matt. 5. 14). And so Hermas in *Sim.* ix. makes the gate of the tower brighter than the sun (2. 2), and the building and all its stones bright as the sun (17. 3—4): the tower foursquare, and its stones foursquare: its foundation stones unhewn, in order that its Foundation may be unhewn (p. 31). In like manner, as we have seen in *Sim.* v. 6 and Clem. Rom. II. 9, the flesh of members of Christ is a temple of God, as the flesh of Christ is the temple of God (Joh. 2. 21). This principle explains some other things in the *Shepherd*,

---

* Dr Sanday, in the *Expositor* for December 1891 (p. 412), describes this reading as "known to several of the Latin Fathers, Irenaeus (twice), Tertullian (three times), and Ambrose and Augustine (once each), and found also in Cod. Veronensis (*b*) of the Old Latin." He also shews traces of it in Justin Martyr's *Apol.* I. 32 and *Dial.* 54. 63. 76.

as we shall see forthwith. The use of verse 13 by Irenaeus suggests that Hermas may have had it in mind when he wrote in *Sim.* ix., Some stones were being added to the building *by the men*, and did not become bright (4. 6); for such as are born "of the will of man" cannot become "children of God."

33—34] The Spirit descending and *remaining* on Jesus was a sign to the Baptist that He was the Son of God. Now in *Sim.* ix. 6 the twelve virgins, on the approach of the Lord of the tower, run to him, attach themselves closely to him, and begin to walk near him round the tower. This adhesion of the virgins, if they be the Holy Ghost, to the tall man who overtops the tower ought to designate him as the Son of God; and accordingly it is said of him in the interpretation of incident, *The glorious man is the Son of God* (12. 8). The like behaviour of the virgins to Hermas (11. 4) illustrates the principle just enunciated, that as He is, so (in their measure) are His members: the Spirit of truth abides with them, as with the Son of God. He abides with the Foundation and with its component parts, of which it is said, They first wore *these spirits;* and they departed not at all from one another, neither the spirits from the men, nor the men from the spirits; but the spirits remained with them till their last sleep, and but for this they would not have been of use for the building of the tower (15. 6). Inseparable from the tower, which is both the Church, or Christ, and the aggregate of the children of God, are the seven women, who are the sevenfold Spirit of God, in *Vis.* iii., and the twelve virgins in *Sim.* ix., who stand round about the tower as its warders, under strict injunctions not to depart from it (5. 1); and round the gate (4. 1), which is again the Son of God.

51] The Son of man is, even to the angels of God, the way between heaven and earth, the realisation of the dream of Jacob (Gen. 28. 12). The preternaturally tall man in *Sim.* ix. 6, who is the Son of God (12. 8), corresponds to the Evangelist's divine Son of man; and at the same time to the Talmudic first Adam, who extended from the earth to the firmament*, and was thus a Jacob's ladder, whose head was in heaven. The colossal man, if not a ladder to the angels, is their "gate of heaven," and thus stands in much the same relation to them as the Son of man in the Gospel. The Lord (writes Hermas) is encompassed by angels as a wall, the gate in which is the Son of God. He is the one entrance to the Lord;

---

* Talm. Bab. *Chagigah* 12 *a*, p. 58 ed. Streane (Camb. 1891).

and not even the most glorious angels can come unto God except through Him (12. 6—8).

Chap. ii. 6 *And there were set there six waterpots of stone, after the manner of the purifying of the Jews, containing two or three firkins apiece.* 7 *Jesus saith unto them, Fill the waterpots with water. And they filled them up to the brim.* 8 *And he saith unto them, Draw out now, and bear unto the governor of the feast.* 10 *Every man at the beginning doth set forth good wine...but thou hast kept the good wine until now.* 19 *Destroy this temple, and in three days I will raise it up.* 21 *But he spake of the temple of his body.*

6—10] The miracle of the Water made Wine is made a parable by Hermas. The large waterpots, at first partly empty, are *filled* to the brim; and their contents are then found to be *good wine*. Accordingly Hermas writes in *Mand.* xii., For the devil tempts the servants of God, and if he find them empty, corrupts them. When a man has *filled* ($\gamma\epsilon\mu\acute{\iota}\sigma\eta$) a great abundance of jars with *good wine*, if there be a few half empty among them, when he comes to the jars, he does not examine the full ones, but only the empty ones; for these soon turn sour, and the flavour of the wine is lost. So when the devil tempts the servants of God, he finds no place to enter them that are full in the faith; but he enters into the empty, and works his will with them, and they become subservient unto him (5. 2—4).

19—21] In Clem. Rom. II. 9 it was said, *We ought to guard the flesh as a temple of God*, and further, that Christ, being first Spirit, *became flesh* (p. 73). If the writer thus associates the idea that the *flesh* is a temple of God with the prologue of S. John's Gospel, we may think that the word *temple* was suggested to him as much by the phrase *the temple of his body* in Joh. 2. 21 as by 1 Cor. 6. 19.

Chap. iii. 3 *Except a man be born again, he cannot see the kingdom of God. 5 Except a man be born of water and of the Spirit, he cannot enter into the kingdom of God. 12 If I have told you earthly things, and ye believe not, how shall ye believe, if I tell you of heavenly things? 13 And no man hath ascended up to heaven, but he that came down from heaven. 14 And as Moses lifted up the serpent in the wilderness, even so must the Son of man be lifted up. 31 He that cometh from above is above all: he that is of the earth is earthly, and speaketh of the earth.*

3] As Moses merely saw the promised land from

Pisgah (Deut. 34. 4), and as others of old saw the promises afar off; so Hermas takes *seeing* literally, and plays thus upon the distinction between seeing and entering into the kingdom of God in *Sim.* ix., He who wears the names of the virgins and the name of the Son of God shall be able to *enter into the kingdom of God.* But the servant of God who wears the names of the women in black shall *see the kingdom of God*, but shall not enter into it (15. 2—3).

5] And why (asks Hermas) did the foundation stones come up from the deep wearing *these spirits?* It was necessary that they should come up through *water*, that they might be made alive; for they could not otherwise *enter into the kingdom of God &c.* Before a man wears the name of the Son of God he is dead; but when he has received the seal, he puts off the deadness and receives back the life. Now the seal is the water: into this they go down dead, and they come up from it alive (16. 1—4). Thus water and "these spirits," the Holy Spirit of the virgins, are the means by which men must be born again.

12, 13, 31] Hermas dwells upon the distinction between things *earthly* and things *from above.* Faith, he says in *Mand.* ix. 11, is from above, from the Lord, and hath great power; but doublemindedness is an earthly spirit and from the devil [Jas. 3. 15], and hath not power. *Mand.* xi. 6 describes the spirit of the *false prophet* as *earthly*, and speaking according to the desires of men, that is "of the earth," and only when interrogated. Lower down we read, with allusion to 1 Joh. 4. 1, *Try* the claimant to inspiration by his life and works, and *believe the Spirit* that comes *from God* and hath power. Hear this parable which I will tell thee. Throw a stone at the heaven and see if thou canst strike it; or pump at it with a water siphon, and see if thou canst bore it. As these things are beyond men's power, so earthly spirits are without power and weak. But see the power that cometh from above. Hail is the least of granules, but when it falls *upon the head* of a man, how it pains him. Or take the *drop* (σταγών) that falls from the roof to the ground, and bores through stone. Thou seest that the least things falling from above to the earth have great power. So too the Divine Spirit *coming from above* is powerful. This Spirit then believe thou, and from the other keep away (16—20).

That drops of water bore into hard stone was a very ancient adage, to which Hermas gives a fresh application. Water being a familiar symbol of the Spirit, he makes *dropping* water a symbol of the Spirit coming from above; with allusion as we may suppose to baptism, both here and in the *dropping* (στάξαντος) of righteousness upon the children of the Church in *Vis.* iii. 9. 1. Compare the rules for baptism in chap. 7 of the *Teaching*. The normal form of it being by immersion in living water, if such water be not accessible, the use of other water is sanctioned. *And if thou have not either, pour out water thrice upon the head, unto the name of Father and Son and Holy Ghost.* The instruction to pour-*out*, namely from the hand or from some vessel, is very suggestive of the outpouring of the Holy Spirit, as in Acts 2. 17, *I will pour out of my Spirit upon all flesh*, and Tit. 3. 5—6, *By the washing of regeneration, and renewing of the Holy Ghost, which he poured out upon us.* Thus the *Didaché* by its word ἔκχεον teaches implicitly that the baptismal water dropping *upon the head* of a man represents the Spirit descending upon him.

14] Searching the *Shepherd* for traces of the sign of *outspreading*, the sign of the Cross, in the *Teaching* (p. 50), I first noticed the dragon of tribulation's *extension* of itself upon the ground, which seemed to be a counterpart of the "sign of the truth" in heaven. This was eventually found to be confirmed by the saying on the serpent in the Fourth Gospel, and further by chap. xxi. 18, which will be commented upon in its place. The encounter of Hermas with the beast, which prefigured the coming tribulation, is described in *Vis.* iv. He was glorifying and giving thanks to God, when a voice replied, Be not double-minded, Hermas. He went forward a little, and behold dust rising *as it were* to heaven. Were cattle coming? The dust thickened, and he suspected that there was something superhuman. The sun glimmered faintly, and behold a huge beast like a sort of sea-monster, with fiery locusts coming out of its mouth, *a hundred feet long*, and with the horned head of a *cerastes*. He faces it boldly in faith, as it comes on with a whirr as though it could lay a city in ruins; and on his near approach that so great beast *stretches itself out upon the ground*, and it did nothing but put out its tongue till he had passed by (1. 4—9). This beast may be an amalgam of different animals, like the beast of Rev. 13. 1 sq., which had seven heads and ten horns, and was like a leopard, and had the feet of a bear, and the mouth of a lion, with power given him by the dragon. It may therefore allude to the "whale" of Jonah (p. 47), and to other things besides. The dust rising *as it were* to heaven, like the stone thrown at the heaven but failing to reach it, in *Mand.* xi. 18, implies vain assumption and essential earthliness. The phrase *upon the ground* is also significant, as it is in *Sim.* ix. 14. 4, where it is asked, why the tower was built *not upon the ground* but upon the rock and upon the gate. The length *a hundred feet* gives the idea of a great serpent; and the further thought then suggests itself that there is an allusion to the words spoken to the serpent in Gen. 3. 14, "Upon thy belly shalt thou go, and dust shalt thou eat all the days of thy life." The *Teaching* had suggested that the beast's *extension of itself* was in the form of a cross. But *as Moses lifted up*, or impaled, or crucified, *the serpent in the wilderness, even so* (it is written) *must the Son of man be lifted up*, or crucified. This suggests that *Vis.* iv. alludes also to the "lifting up" of the serpent of Moses, with which it was natural to associate the serpent of Eve. Thus the Gospel and the *Teaching* point to the same interpretation of the gesture of the beast on the approach of Hermas. The author of the *Shepherd* may have referred to verse 14 merely as recording the act of Moses. The serpent of Hermas was *able to destroy peoples* (2. 3), as the serpents in the wilderness slew *much people* (Numb. 21. 6). The *Teaching* predicts that the world-deceiver will appear *as Son of God.* In Lagarde's *Hippol. quae feruntur* 14. 20 (1858) the assimilation is extended to all particulars, so that *as the Christ gave to believers upon him the precious and vivifying Cross, the deceiver will likewise give his own Sign.*

Two features of the beast call for further remark. Its head, according to the manuscripts, was like *a tile*, or "pottery," for which Hilgenfeld reads conjecturally, like that *of a cerastes*. This word means a horned serpent in Prov. 23. 32, and it is an epithet of a bullock "that hath horns" in Ps. 69. 31. It was likely, for reasons to which it would be inappropriate to digress now, that Hermas would allude to the horned beast of Dan. 7. 7; and this is of itself a reason for adopting the simple and sound emendation, κεράστου for κεράμου. And the length of the beast being *a hundred* feet, if we suppose this number to be significant, like the number of the beast in the Apocalypse, then, since the letter R in Greek is the figure for a hundred, we have at once an allusion to Rome, which in fact lies so near the surface that Hermas cannot have failed to notice it, and must therefore have intended it. Examples of the uniliteral acrostic abound in the *Sibylline Oracles*, in one place of which (xi. 114) the number a hundred designates both Romulus and Remus. The enormous bulk and brute force of the beast, its horned head, and its prefigurement of persecution all point to imperial Rome.

Chap. iv. 6 *Jesus therefore, being wearied with his journey, sat thus on the well.* 15 *Sir, give me this water, that I thirst not, neither come hither to draw.* 24 *God is a Spirit: and they that worship him must worship him in spirit and in truth.* 34 *My meat is to do the will of him that sent me, and to finish his work.* 36 *And he that reapeth receiveth wages, and gathereth fruit unto life eternal.*

6, 15] In the explanation of the parable of the Vineyard in *Sim.* v. it is said that the Son himself cleansed the sins of the people of God, *having toiled much and endured many toils* (6. 2); where *toiled* may have been suggested by the fact that Jesus was physically wearied or *toil-worn* (ver. 6). The word for *endure* (ἀντλεῖν) is used, but in a different sense, in this chapter and chap. ii. of S. John's Gospel.

24] *God is a Spirit* or *God is Spirit*. If "the Word was God," and "God is Spirit," the Word (or Christ) preexisted as Spirit, according to Clem. Rom. II. 1, 9 and *Sim.* v. 6 (p. 73). When it is said, as it is often said, that Hermas confounds the Persons of the Son and the Spirit, it should be remarked that he places himself in a dilemma by making the householder, the slave, and the son in the parable of the Vineyard play the parts of the Father, the Son, and the Holy Ghost respectively; for by keeping the three absolutely separate he would have fallen into an opposite heresy, and failed again to represent the "Trinity in Unity." Due allowance must be made for the necessary incompleteness of any such parable, and especially of the representation of the Spirit in a bodily, human shape. With *Sim.* ix. 1. 1 compare 2 Cor. 3. 17, *The Lord is the Spirit.*

In spirit and in truth &c. Is this combination of spirit and truth traceable in Hermas? There are sayings on truth in *Mand.* iii. which are allowed to be akin to sayings of or recorded by S. John: *Again he saith to me, Love truth, and let all truth proceed out of thy mouth, that the Spirit which God made to dwell in this flesh may be found truthful with all men; and thus the Lord that dwelleth in thee shall be glorified. For the Lord is true* (ἀληθινός) *in every word, and with him is no lie....Thou, saith he, thinkest well and truly; for thou oughtest as a servant of God to walk in truth, and an evil conscience ought not to dwell with the Spirit of truth* (1, 4). Notice the word ἀληθινός, which is much used by S. John: the

form of expression "true, and no lie," comparing
1 Joh. 2. 27: the phrase "to walk in truth," comparing the nearly identical phrase in 2 Joh. 4 and
3 Joh. 3: and the expression "Spirit of truth," which
is found only in the Fourth Gospel and 1 Joh. 4. 6 in
the New Testament. To all this add the requirement
of truth in *the spirit* which God has "made to dwell in
this flesh," that so the Lord which dwelleth in thee
may "be glorified;" and we have in the citation from
Mand. iii., as a paraphrase of the saying of which
traces were sought, *The servant of God must glorify
Him in spirit and in truth.*

34] In the parable of the Vineyard in *Sim.* v.,
a certain man had a field and many slaves; and
part of the field he planted as a vineyard, and he put
a trusty and well-pleasing slave in charge of it, with
orders merely to stake it, and went on a journey.
The slave did as he was bidden, and then said, *I
have finished this commandment of the Lord*, now
I will also dig the vineyard: he digged it, and
plucked out the weeds, and the Master on his return
rejoiced greatly at the works of the slave: and he
told his beloved son and his counsellors what he had
commanded, and what he had found done, and they
rejoiced with the slave at *the witness which the Master*

witnessed unto him (Joh. 5. 32). After some days the Master of the house made a supper, and sent the slave many *meats* (ἐδέσματα) from it; and the slave kept a bare sufficiency for himself, and *distributed* the rest to his fellow slaves (2. 1—9). The field is this world, the weeds are the iniquities of the people of God, the slave is the Son of God, and *the meats are the commandments which God gave through His Son* (5. 2—3). The *meat* (βρῶμα) of Jesus was to do the will of the Father, and to *finish* His work: the *meats* sent to the servant who personates the Son of God in the parable, and *distributed* (Joh. 6. 11) by him to his fellow servants, are said by the Shepherd to be *the commandments which God gave through His Son*, according to Joh. 10. 18; 12. 49; 13. 34.

36] The reaper's gathering *fruit unto life eternal* is reproduced in *Sim.* iv., Do thou therefore bear fruit, that in that summer thy fruit may be known. These things therefore if thou do, thou canst bear *fruit unto the world to come* (5, 7).

Chap. v. 3 *In these lay a great multitude of impotent folk, of blind, halt, withered.* 5 *And a certain man was there, which had an infirmity thirty and eight years.* 6 *Wilt thou be made whole?* 7 *Sir, I have no man, when the water is troubled, to cast me into the pool: but while I am coming, another goeth down before me.* 14 *Behold, thou art made whole: sin no more, lest a worse thing come upon thee.* 21...*even so the Son quickeneth whom he will.* 24 *He that heareth my word...hath everlasting life.* 32 *There is another that beareth witness of me; and I know that the witness which he witnesseth of me is true.* 39 *Search the Scriptures &c.* 40 *And ye will not come to me, that ye may have life.*

3.—7] With these verses we have compared the *Shepherd's* picture of the faulty stones lying round about the tower, waiting to be hewn and cast into the building (p. 45). The word *whole* or sound in the New Testament always implies a work of healing, except in the phrase "sound speech" in Tit. 2. 8. In *Sim.* viii. r. 3 sq. it is used of the Great Willow, which remained miraculously whole when so many branches had been cut from it; and in *Sim.* ix. of stones healed by hewing, and so made fit to be facing stones of the tower (8. 5).

14] *Sin no more* comes as a surprise, after the record of a miracle of healing which seems to imply nothing more than bodily *infirmity*. The saying, whether here only or in a later verse also, had made an impression upon Hermas, who most strongly urges the duty which it inculcates. In *Mand.* iv. the

Shepherd counsels a certain tolerance in the treatment of those who have once fallen, not to encourage delinquency, but in order that he who has sinned may *sin no more*. Of his former sin there is one that can give healing (1. 11). Have I heard rightly (asks Hermas) that there is no repentance after that when we *went down into water* and received remission of our former sins? Yes, for he who has received remission of sins must *sin no more* (3. 1—2). To *go-down* into the water is to be baptized. Compare *Sim.* ix. 16. 4, *Into the water then they go-down dead, and they come up alive;* *Epist. Barn.* 11. 8, 11; and Acts 8. 38. If to *go-down* into the water, with or without mention of "baptism," meant to be baptized, Hermas may have taken the goings down into the pool of Bethesda in that sense. Then, applying *Sin no more* to those who went down (ver. 7), he would have inferred that they received remission of sins once for all. The impotent man's infirmity suggests men's *infirmity* against the wiliness of the devil, as in *Mand.* iv. 3. 4. It was to be expected that Hermas, if he noticed the cures at Bethesda, would take a hint from "Sin no more," and convert them into cases of the *healing of sin*. The expression has a scriptural basis, and the idea pervades the *Shepherd*.

The thought that sin in general is a malady to be

cured leads up to the thought of sin incurable, which is *sin unto death* and *blasphemy against the Holy Ghost*, according to S. John and the Synoptic Gospels respectively. Of such sin under its various names there are traces in the Mandates and Similitudes of Hermas. In *Mand.* v. we read, Sharp temper, at first merely senseless, engenders bitterness, anger, rage, fury, which *becomes sin great and incurable.* For when these spirits dwell in one vessel, where also the Holy Spirit dwells, it becomes over full, and *the Holy Spirit departs* from the man...But refrain from temper; and if thou keep this commandment, thou shalt be able to keep all the rest which I shall command thee (2. 4—8). In *Sim.* vi. it is said, of the erring sheep shepherded by the angel of luxury, For they forget the commandments of the living God, and walk in vain deceits and luxuries, and are destroyed by this angel, *some to death and some to corruption.* In some (it is explained) there is no repentance unto life, because they added to their other sins that they *blasphemed against the name of the Lord.* Such men therefore are εἰς θάνατον, *to death.* But those who, however corrupted from the truth, did not blaspheme at all against the Lord, have hope of repentance whereby they may live. Corruption then hath hope of some renewal, but death hath eternal destruction (2. 2—4). In *Sim.* viii. it is said of those whose rods were found dry and moth eaten, These are the apostates and betrayers of the Church, and they that *blasphemed the Lord in their sins*, and furthermore were ashamed of the name of the Lord by which they were called. These therefore utterly perished unto God (6. 4). Of those whose rods were half green and half dry, many, when they heard the commandments of the angel of repentance, repented. But some of them apostatised utterly. These have no repentance; for on account of their transactions they *blasphemed the Lord* and denied Him (8. 1—2). In *Sim.* ix. in like manner it is said, From the black mountain the believers are apostates, *blasphemers against the Lord*, betrayers of the servants of God. For them there is not repentance, but death (19. 1). In these passages we have the idea of a *sin of blasphemy*, which cannot be repented of and forgiven: a *sin against the Holy Ghost*, whom it grieves and makes to depart from a man: a *sin unto death* and everlasting destruction: a *sin* incurable, and therefore *eternal*, according to S. Mark 3. 29, *But whosoever shall blaspheme against the Holy Spirit hath never forgiveness, but is guilty of an eternal sin* (R. V.). On "sin unto death" in the First Epistle of S. John see Bp Westcott's notes, comparing with the *Shepherd's* "some to death and some to corruption" the words from Origen's *Hom. in Ex.* x. 3, "There are some sins which are *ad damnum*...some *ad interitum.*"

21, 24] The word *quicken* or make alive is used in *Mand.* iv., I was quickened on hearing these things from thee thus exactly (3. 7); where the turn of expression was possibly suggested by verse 24, *He that heareth my words &c.*, in connexion with verse 21. It is also used in *Sim.* ix. 16. 2 of the quickening or new birth through baptism. *Whom he will* is illustrated by *Sim.* ix. 9. 3, where it is said to the Lord of the tower, who insists that some of the fine, round stones must be made use of, If, Sir, there is necessity, why vex thyself, and not choose for the building *whom* (what stones) *thou wilt?*

32] The noun and the verb *witness* are predominantly Johannine in the New Testament, and their combination in this verse (cf. Rev. 1. 2) would have suggested the *witness-witnessed* by the Master to the slave who personates the Son of God in the parable of the Vineyard in *Sim.* v. (p. 90).

39—40] *Search ye* (or *Ye search*) *the scriptures.* It is against the principle of Hermas to allude plainly to the Scriptures; but in *Mand.* x. he writes, that men who merely believe, and have never *searched* and investigated concerning the truth and divine things, but give their whole minds to money making and the affairs of the world, lose the spiritual sense, and grow barren, like neglected vineyards (1. 4—6). *Sim.* x. teaches, Whosoever do his commandments *shall have life.* But all who keep them not *flee from their life and turn away from him* (2. 4): they will not come unto him who is "the life" that they may have life. The simple phrase " have *life*," without qualification, points to the Fourth Gospel.

Chap. vi. 11 *And Jesus took the loaves; and when he had given thanks, he distributed to the disciples.* 27 *Work not for the meat which perisheth, but for that meat which endureth unto everlasting life, which the Son of man shall give unto you: for him hath God the Father sealed.* 28 *Then said they unto him, What shall we do, that we might work the works of God?* 29 *Jesus answered and said unto them, This is the work of God, that ye believe on him whom he hath sent.* 44 *No man can come to me, except the Father which hath sent me draw him: and I will raise him up at the last day.* 47 *He that believeth on me hath everlasting life.* 48 *I am the bread of life.* 63 *The words that I speak unto you, they are spirit, and they are life.* 70 *Have I not chosen you twelve, and one of you is a devil?* 71 *He spake of Judas...for he it was that should betray him, being one of the twelve.*

11, 27] As Jesus *distributed* the loaves for the feeding of the Five Thousand, so (as we have seen) the slave who represents the Son of God in the parable of the Vineyard in *Sim.* v. *distributed* the meats sent to him from the Master's table, which were the commandments of God, to his fellowservants (p. 90). The meats in the parable are interpreted according to the saying of Jesus, *My meat is to do the will of him that sent me, and to finish his work* (Joh. 4. 34). In this chapter likewise, from verse 27 onwards, He spiritualises the idea of *meat* or *bread*; which would have led Hermas to do the same in the preceding verses, and spiritualise the loaves for the feeding of the multitude. This enhances the significance of his use of the word *distributed*, and justifies the opinion that he took it from the account of the miracle. *The meat which endureth unto everlasting life* being the commandments of God, we see an allusion to verse 27 in *Vis.* ii., These things have saved thee, if thou abide in them; and they save all that *work* such things, and walk in guilelessness and simplicity. These prevail over all wickedness, and shall *endure unto everlasting life* (3. 2). With the sealing of the Son of man by God contrast the *seal of the Son of God* in *Sim.* ix. 31. 4.

28—29, 47] As in the Gospel to *work the works of God* is to *believe on him whom He hath sent*, so Hermas identifies the former duty with the operation of faith, and writes in *Sim.* i. 7, *Work ye the works of God, remembering his commandments and the promises which He promised, and believe him that He will do them if his commandments be kept.* The essence of *Mand.* i. is *Believe* (1 Joh. 3. 23); and it is said that he who keeps it shall "live unto God." Compare *Mand.* xii. 3. 1, *Work truth, faith &c., and thou shalt live unto him*; noticing the phrase "work truth," which is but slightly varied from *do the truth* in chap. iii. 21 and 1 Joh. 1. 6. See also in 1 Joh. 2. 25 and *Vis.* i. 3. 4, *the promise which He promised*, comparing the phrases to *work works* (Joh. 9. 4) and *witness witness* (p. 95) in S. John and Hermas.

44, 48, 63] Peculiar to S. John in the New Testament is the phrase the *last day* (sing.), which Hermas uses in *Vis.* ii., But for the Gentiles there is repentance until the *last day* (2. 5); and in *Vis.* iii.,

He expecteth nothing but the *last day* of his life (12. 2). The idea of the saying, *I am the bread of life*, may be resolved into two parts: first, the Torah or Law, the sum of the commandments of God, is the true bread; and next the Son of God is the embodiment of the Law, and therefore Himself the true bread, the bread of life. The former thought has been sufficiently dwelt upon in connexion with *Sim.* v. As to the latter, Hermas in *Sim.* viii. 3. 2 sq. makes the great willow mean "the law of God given to the whole world," adding that *This law is the Son of God preached to the ends of the earth;* and he speaks of such as had *pleased* (εὐηρέστησαν) *the law* and kept it, remembering his attribution of a divine personality to the law. *The words that I speak unto you are life* may have suggested in *Sim.* ix. 21. 2, Their words only live, but their works are dead (Heb. 6. 1).

54—58] The word τρώγειν, *to eat*, which occurs four times in these verses, is used in *Sim.* v. 3. 7.

70—71] Judas, the son of Simon Iscariot, the betrayer being, as remarked by the four Evangelists, *one of the twelve*, Hermas peoples one of his twelve mountains, the black one, the first "which shall be last," with apostates, blasphemers of the Lord, and betrayers of the servants of God (*Sim.* ix. 19).

Chap. vii. 28 *But he that sent me is true.*

In the Gospels the word ἀληθινός is used once by S. Luke, of the *true* mammon, and nine times by S. John. It is used once in 1 Thess. 1. 9, three or four times in the Epistle to the Hebrews, and fourteen times in the Apocalypse and First Epistle of John. Thus it is so far characteristic of S. John that its use would have been suggested by an acquaintance with his writings. Hermas (as we have seen) uses it in *Mand.* iii. 1 as an epithet of the Lord: he uses it also in *Vis.* iii. 7. 1, where he writes, *their true way*, as a variation upon "the way of truth," probably under the influence of the Fourth Gospel.

Chap. viii. 3 *And the scribes and Pharisees brought unto him a woman taken in adultery. 7 So when they continued asking him, he...said unto them, He that is without sin among you, let him first cast a stone at her. 11 And Jesus said unto her, Neither do I condemn thee: go, and sin no more. 32 The truth shall make you free. 41 Ye do the deeds of your father. 44 Ye are of your father the devil.*

The Shepherd in *Mand.* iv. charges a man to keep purity, and not to harbour thoughts about his neighbour's wife, or about any act of fornication, or any evil practices like to such things (1. 1). I say to him, Sir, suffer me to ask thee a few things. If one that hath a wife who is faithful in the Lord find her in some adultery, doth the man sin in living with her? It was no sin so long as he was in ignorance; but when he has learned the fact, if she repent not, he becomes a partner in her adultery if he continues to live with her (1. 5). What then must he do? Let him put her away and abide alone. But if she repent after being put away, and desire to return to her own husband, shall she not be received? Certainly if the husband receive her not he sinneth. He that hath sinned and repents should be received; *yet not repeatedly, for to the servants of God there is but one repentance* (1. 8). The case of man and wife is said to be typical. *Not only is it adultery to defile the flesh, but also to do things like the Gentiles.* The Shepherd adds that he counsels condonation of a first offence, not by way of giving occasion for sin, but *in order that he who has sinned may sin no more* (1. 11).

3, 7, 11] The pericope of the Woman taken in Adultery supplies a basis for this teaching of *Mand.* iv., which supposes the case of *a woman found in some adultery*. Hermas, like the scribes and Pharisees, *continues asking* about the case; and the Shepherd in reply says in effect that he who casts the first stone, the husband who disallows the wife's repentance, is not without sin. The Shepherd, like Jesus, does not finally condemn the sinner for one sin, but would have him *sin no more*. He allows repentance, but once only, and he defends his lenience as the best means of securing that he who has sinned shall sin no more: *he* (not *she*), for the reason given below.

Tertullian in *De Pudicit.* 21 admits that the Church has power to forgive a sin; but he deprecates its use, lest men should sin more. Thus while, as befits a Montanist, he denounces the *Shepherd of Hermas* for its lack of severity, he differs from it not so much in theory, as on the question what it is expedient to allow in practice. But in judging of Hermas it is essential to notice that, after his manner, he spiritualises the special case of the woman found in adultery, and gives the sin of the *adulteress* a very wide connotation, making it the type of all manner of heathen living and worldliness. The conclusion of the whole matter with him is that *he*, τὸν ἡμαρτηκότα, the sinner generally, should sin no more. The woman that is a sinner has the same typical character in the *Shepherd* as in Jas. 4. 4, *Ye adulteresses, know ye not that the friendship of the world is enmity with God?*

To this verse, where alone in the whole New Testament the word φιλία, *friendship*, occurs, Hermas alludes in *Mand.* x., speaking of otiose believers as blinded to the things of God by worldly business and wealth and *Gentile friendships* (1. 4). Adultery, the old-world symbol of idolatry, appropriated to itself those extensions of meaning which had been read into "idolatry" itself. Compare in Mark 8. 38, *this adulterous and sinful generation;* and 1 Joh. 5. 21, *Little children, keep yourselves from idols.* There remains the question, which we must leave to the judgment of the reader, whether Hermas, if he knew the pericope of the Woman taken in Adultery, knew it as part of the Fourth Gospel or of some other writing*.

32—34] *The truth shall make you free...He that doeth sin is a servant of sin.* The thought of these

---

* In his *Study of Codex Bezae* (1891) in the Cambridge *Texts and Studies* Professor J. R. Harris, who supposes the pericope to have been expunged from copies of the Gospel through Montanist influence, finds traces of it in the *Cod. Bez.* text of Acts 5. 18 sq. and in the Shepherd's μηκέτι ἁμαρτάνειν (p. 195). The *Cod. Bez.* text of Acts 1. 2 (*ib.* p. 154) runs thus in the Latin (and correspondingly in the Greek), *usque in eum diem quem susceptus est, quo praecepit apostolis per Spm. Sanctum quos elegit, et praecepit praedicare evangelium;* where *et praecepit &c.* must have been interpolated from Mark 16. 15, 19, the sole authority for the combination of the statement ἀνελήμφθη with the command κηρύξατε τὸ εὐαγγέλιον. On Acts 1. 2 see also Tischendorf's *Nov. Test. Graece.*

verses, with or without vestige of their form, should be discoverable in the *Shepherd*. That true freedom is independence of the lower self was a maxim of religion and philosophy. Aristotle speaks of servitude to pleasures; and Hermas in *Mand.* xii. writes, If thou *serve* (δουλεύσῃς) the Good Desire and submit thyself to it, thou shalt be able to have dominion over the Evil Desire and subdue it (2. 5). Thus he says of the good principle, *Cui servire regnare*, "whose service is perfect freedom." Such freedom comes of serving the Spirit (*Sim.* v. 6. 5), which is to serve God and walk *in truth* (*Mand.* iii. 4). To swerve from *the truth* because of its purity is to follow evil desires (*Vis.* iii. 7. 3), and "they that plan evil in their hearts draw death and *captivity* upon themselves" (i. 1. 8). Here, for the sense, some compare these verses; to which (we may add) Iren. I. 1. 6 perhaps refers by the expression *lead captive* (Rom. 7. 23) *from the truth*. The phrase to *know the truth* (ver. 32) is found in *Vis.* iii. 6. 2 (2 Joh. 1). To the servant in *Sim.* v. it is said (2. 2, 7), Keep my commandment and *thou shalt be free with me* (ver. 36).

41, 44] The angel of righteousness teaches in *Mand.* xii. 6. 2 that by returning to God men may overmaster *the works of the devil* (1 Joh. 3. 8).

Chap. ix. 1 *And as he passed by, he saw a man blind from his birth.* 3 *Neither hath this man sinned, nor his parents: but that the works of God should be manifest in him.* 4 *I must work the works of him that sent me, while it is day.* 24 *Give glory to God.*

1—3, 24] Sayings in this chapter associate sin with blindness, in a way to suggest the expression of deliverance from sin in terms of the "recovering of sight to the blind" (Luke 4. 18), as in Clem. Rom. II. 9 (p. 72), *In what but in this flesh did we recover sight?* Here the homilist spiritualises miracles of recovery of sight in the flesh, and among them doubtless the case of the man *blind from birth.* To this he seems to allude in his first chapter also, which has points of contact with the ninth, when he writes, *What praise should we give Him* or reward in recompense for what we received? *Being* mentally *blind* (πηροί)...*we recovered sight.* The simple word "being" expresses being by nature and "from birth," and the word πηρός may be a substitute for S. John's τυφλός, *blind* (ver. 1), as it is in some early writings quoted in Resch's *Agrapha* § 4, p. 24 (1889); the man that was blind from birth being called "πηρός from birth" in *Clem. Hom.* XIX. 22 and *Apost. Const.* v. 7, while Justin Martyr uses the phrase in the plural in *Apol.*

1. 22, and again in *Dial.* 69, *them that were from birth and according to the flesh* πηρούς. If Clem. Rom. II. was thinking of the miracle in question, what he says of *giving praise to God* for opening the eyes of the mind (chaps. 1, 9) would be accounted for by verse 24, *Give glory to God.* Hermas in *Mand.* v. speaks of the passionate as *blinded*, and of patience as *glorifying the Lord* at all seasons (2. 3, 7). Here and elsewhere, under the figure of spiritual darkening and its antidote (*Mand.* x. 1), he may have been thinking more or less of the cognate Gospel miracles; but the former passage has closer relationship with 1 Joh. 2. 11, *He that hateth his brother is in darkness...the darkness hath blinded his eyes.*

3—6] The phrases *works of God* and *work works* are Johannine, and both are used by Hermas. We may notice also that the word χαμαί, *on the ground*, is found in the New Testament only in ver. 6 and chap. xviii. 6, *They went backward, and fell to the ground;* and that it is an emphatic word with Hermas, who uses it of the dragon of tribulation which extends itself *upon the ground*, and of the tower as built upon the rock, and not *upon the ground* (p. 85). Compare the parable of the house built upon the rock, and not upon the sand (Matt. 7. 24—26).

Chap. x. 1 *He that entereth not by the door into the sheepfold, but climbeth up some other way, the same is a thief and a robber.* 2 *But he that entereth in by the door is the shepherd of the sheep.* 9 *I am the door: by me if any man enter in, he shall be saved.* 11 *I am the good shepherd: the good shepherd giveth his life for the sheep.* 12 *But he that is an hireling... leaveth the sheep, and fleeth: and the wolf catcheth them, and scattereth the sheep.* 16 *And other sheep I have, which are not of this fold &c.; and there shall be one flock, one shepherd.* 37 *If I do not the works of my Father, believe me not.* 38 *But if I do, though ye believe not me, believe the works.*

1—9] In *Sim.* ix. the *gate*, which was newly cut out of the rock (2. 2), is the Son of God manifest in the flesh (12. 1—3). It has been argued that this cannot refer to the saying *I am the door* (ver. 9), the change of word from θύρα in the Gospel to πύλη in the similitude being thought to be an insuperable difficulty. But since Hermas systematically disguises his allusions, one of his artifices being to replace a word in its proper connexion by some synonym; it would have been quite after his manner, in working up the parable of the Good Shepherd, to write *gate* for *door*, not altogether omitting the latter word, but using it in *Vis.* iii., And ye be shut out with your goods outside *the door* [Matt. 25. 10] of the tower (9. 6). This he might have done merely to veil his allusion; as in *Vis.* iii. 13, seemingly for no other reason, he writes *straightway forgetteth*, instead of *remembereth no more* (p. 8). But the word *gate* may have been preferred as more congruous with its surroundings in *Sim.* ix., and as the resultant of allusions at once to the *door*, the Son of God, and to passages which use the figure of the *gate*. On the whole, the change of word counts for little in Hermas; the real question being whether a connexion can be made out between the contexts of *door* and *gate* in the Fourth Gospel and the *Shepherd* respectively. Now in the Gospel we read, *I am the door: by me if any man enter in, he shall be saved;* to which corresponds very closely in *Sim.* ix., as Zahn has remarked, The gate was made new, *that those who were to be saved might enter by it* (12. 3). And not only so, but as the Gospel recognises other possible ways of entry than by the door (ver. 1), Hermas accordingly makes some stones find a temporary lodgment in the tower, which have not been carried through the gate by the hands of the virgins (4. 8). Thus it appears that the gate is a transfiguration of the door.

2, 12, 16] Some of the various shepherds in Hermas have traits taken from passages of Holy Writ, including the section on the Good Shepherd. In *Sim.* vi. the angel of retribution is depicted as a *great shepherd* (2. 5), and he and others were called the *shepherds of the sheep* (1. 5), with twofold reference perhaps to the "shepherd of the sheep" in verse 2, and the "great shepherd of the sheep" in Heb. 13. 20. The Good Shepherd is also the Lord of scattered flocks, which he purposes to unite in one under one shepherd. Hermas in *Sim.* ix. supposes a Lord of flocks tended by a plurality of shepherds. If when he comes (1 Pet. 5. 4) he should find some of the sheep scattered, woe to the shepherds; but if the very shepherds be scattered, what shall they answer him for the flocks? Will they say that they were worried by the flocks? They would not be believed, for it is a thing incredible that a shepherd would be harmed by sheep: he would only be the more punished for his mendacity. And I am a Shepherd, and am under the strongest obligation to give account concerning you (31. 4—6). This may be accounted for as an adaptation of sayings of the Good Shepherd to the schisms of unworthy overseers (Acts 20. 28 sq.), which rend the flock; the shepherds, not the sheep as in the *Teaching* (chap. 16), being "turned to wolves." The phrase to *feed sheep*, used in *Sim.* vi. 1. 6, occurs in the charge to S. Peter in chap. xxi. 17.

38] *Believe the works* is a unique and remarkable precept, which Hermas makes his own in *Mand.* vi., These then are the works of the angel of righteousness: him therefore *believe* thou and *his works*...The things concerning the faith this commandment sheweth, even that thou shouldest *believe the works* of the angel of righteousness, and do them (2. 3, 10).

Chap. xi. 9 *Are there not twelve hours in the day? If any man walk in the day, he stumbleth not, because he seeth the light of this world.* 10 *But if a man walk in the night, he stumbleth, because there is no light in him.* 11 *Our friend Lazarus sleepeth.* 13 *Howbeit Jesus spake of his death: but they thought that he had spoken of taking of rest in sleep.* 40 *The glory of God.* 48 *If we let him thus alone...the Romans shall come and take away both our place and nation.*

9] First, taking the day to include "the evening and the morning," or leaving the night out of consideration, we find the formula that there are *twelve hours in the day* assumed in the following curious equation of a day of torment to a year in *Sim.* vi.,

The time of luxury is one hour, but an hour of torment has the force of thirty days. If then a man has lived one day in luxury and deceits, and has been tormented one day, the day of torment has the effect of a whole year (4. 4); each of its twelve hours having the force of 30 days, and the twelve together of 360 days.

9—10] He who walks in the light *stumbleth not*: he who walks in the darkness *stumbleth*. *Mand.* vi. 1 teaches that the crooked way of unrighteousness has not paths, but no-ways and many *things-to-stumble-at*, and is rough and thorny; but they who go in the straight way *walk* smoothly and *without-stumbling.* Thus the Lord's sayings on day and night, the seasons of light and darkness, are transferred to the two ways, which were well known to Hermas and to every one as the Way of Light and the Way of Darkness.

13] The substantive κοίμησις, *taking rest* in sleep, being found here only in the Canonical Scriptures (not including Ecclesiasticus), it is of some significance that Hermas uses it in *Vis.* iii. 11. 3, *they are expectant of nothing but their last-sleep;* and in *Sim.* ix. 15. 6, *but the spirits remained with them till their last-sleep.*

40] *The glory of God* is spoken of here and in verse 4, and again in chap. xii. 43, *For they loved the glory of men more than the glory of God.* Hermas in *Vis.* iii. 1. 5 is affrighted when he sees "these things lying, and no one in the place," but he remembers *the glory of God* and takes courage. In *Mand.* xii. 4. 2 it is said to him, Perceivest thou not *the glory of God*, how great and strong and wondrous it is?

48] This mention of *the Romans* stands alone in the Gospels, except that a version of the inscription on the Cross is said to have been in their language. The dragon of persecution in *Sim.* iv. is very suggestive of imperial Rome. If its "number," the Greek R, was meant to point to Rome (p. 86); the question arises, Did Hermas, like Irenaeus (v. 30. 3), know of *Lateinos* (in Greek letters) as one of the solutions of the number of the beast in the Apocalypse?

Chap. xii. 24 *Except a corn of wheat fall into the ground and die, it abideth alone: but if it die, it bringeth forth much fruit.* 28 *Father, glorify thy name. Then came there a voice from heaven &c.* 32 *And I, if I be lifted up from the earth, will draw all men unto me.* 33 *This he said, signifying what death he should die.* 37 *But though he had done so many miracles before them, yet they believed not on him.* 39...*because that Esaias said again,*

40 *He hath blinded their eyes, and hardened their heart.* 41 *These things said Esaias, when he saw his glory, and spake of him.*

24] The Church in *Vis.* i. sits alone upon her chair (2. 2), but in *Vis.* iii. Hermas sits with her upon the bench (2. 4). The false prophet in *Mand.* xi. 1 sits alone upon his chair, while faithful men sit together on the bench. The Church upon her chair was sick and at the point of death: her erect posture in *Vis.* ii. was the sign that she had risen again (p. 8): after her resurrection she has the companionship of Hermas, himself a typical character, and she shews him a vision of the building of the tower, which is again the Church. Thus she claims for herself a countless progeny of living stones (Matt. 3. 9), answering (as stones elsewhere in the *Shepherd* replace seeds) to the much fruit of the corn of wheat which falls into the ground and dies.

28] In *Vis.* ii. 1. 2 Hermas begins to pray to the Lord and *glorify His name;* and when he has made an end the Church is seen and speaks to him. In *Vis.* iii. 4. 3 he is told that it is not because of his great merit that he is chosen to receive revelations (Matt. 11. 25), but *that the name of God may be glorified.* See also *Vis.* iv. 1. 3 and *Sim.* ix. 18. 5.

32—33] As the Cross lifts up Christ, or the *temple of his body* (Joh. 2. 21), so Ignatius makes it lift up the several stones of the spiritual temple; writing in *Ephes.* 9, as rendered by Bp Lightfoot, *But I have learned that certain persons passed through you from yonder, bringing evil doctrine; whom ye suffered not to sow seed in you, for ye stopped your ears, so that ye might not receive the seed sown by them; forasmuch as ye are stones of a temple, which were prepared beforehand for a building of God the Father, being hoisted up to the heights* (ὕψη) *through the engine of Jesus Christ, which is the Cross, and using for a rope the Holy Spirit; while your faith is your windlass, and love is the way that leadeth up to God.* Very like this is the building of the tower upon the rock higher than the mountains in *Sim.* ix. of Hermas. But although the resemblance has been remarked upon in general terms, I do not know that it has been worked out in detail. The points to be noticed are that both writers make the Cross and the Holy Spirit instrumental in the building. Without thinking of Ignatius, and solely from a comparison of the *Shepherd* with the *Teaching*, we found an allusion to the Cross in the spreading out of the hands of the virgins to receive the stones which they were to carry up to the tower; and we made out that the virgins represented the Holy Ghost, who was thus seen to be instrumental in building it. Again, while Ignat. *Ephes.* 9 brings in Faith and Love, Hermas has a string of seven virtues from Faith to Love in *Vis.* iii., and of twelve in *Sim.* ix.; and he concatenates the virtues in each series and makes them inseparable. Of the seven he says that they are "daughters of one another," with Faith for the mother of all; and adds that *their powers are laid hold of by one another and follow one another* (8. 7). Thus they make an endless chain or "rope"; and they stand in a circle round the tower, which is upheld by them, by the command of the Lord (8. 2). Like them are the virgins of *Sim.* ix., who stand round the tower; and they bear, not the whole tower at once, but its stones one by one. The twelve coil themselves round each stone; four strong cardinal virtues standing at the corners, and the rest in pairs between; and so, making themselves a chain, they carry them (4. 1). But to return to the Gospel, it is said, *I will draw all men unto me* (ver. 32), and *No man can come to me, except the Father which hath sent me draw him* (Joh. 6. 44). The drawing might be "with cords of a man, with bands of love" (Hos. 11. 4); or it might be with the cord of the Holy Spirit, of which the holy spirit

Love in Hermas is a partial manifestation. From all this it seems to follow that Hermas borrowed from Ignatius, and both from the Fourth Gospel, in their accounts of the building of the temple or tower.

In Lagarde's *Hippol. R.* 1. 59 (p. 30) the Church is likened to a ship in a storm upon the sea of the world, having Christ for pilot and the Cross for mast, and bound about with ropes of love. It has *angels* for sailors, and the symbol of the Passion as *a ladder that leadeth up to the height, drawing* (ἕλκουσα) the faithful to the ascent of the heavens; where the drawing or attraction of men upwards through the Cross is accounted for by verse 32, and the grouping of *angels, ladder, heaven* in part by chap. i. 51. But the imagery bears the stamp of Ignatius also, who (a century before) had in the same realistic way made the Cross a mechanism for raising men up on high*; and the presumption hence arising that Hippolytus is a witness to Ignatius is strengthened by the consideration that his figure of *ship, storm, pilot* may owe its origin to

---

* Cotelier and later writers on Ignatius add words from Methodius *On the Cross* (Migne *P. G.* 18. 400) to the effect that it is a μηχανή for drawing up *foursquare* stones to be fitted into the building of the Church. The epithet seemed to be from Hermas, and I found in the context the idea of Justin Martyr that *a man spreading his hands is cruciform*, like the virgins as they received the stones in *Sim.* ix. 3. 2 (p. 50). Irenaeus sees the uplifting power of the cross in 2 Kings 6. 6 (Gebh.).

Ignat. *Polyc.* 2. 3, which it has been thought merely to illustrate. Returning to the *Shepherd* and searching it for some form of the word *draw* (ver. 32), we read in *Vis.* iii. 2. 6 (cf. 5. 2) of stones *drawn* (ἑλκομένους) up from the deep and set in the building.

37—40] *Hardening of heart** in the Gospels connotes imperviousness to conviction, with respect to miracles or signs. Here it is said to have entailed incapacity for belief, *though he had done so many signs before them.*. The expression is found again in Mark 3. 5, *Being grieved for the hardness of their hearts, he saith unto the man, Stretch forth thine hand:* Mark 6. 52, *For they understood not concerning the loaves, but their heart was hardened:* and Mark 8. 17—19, *Why reason ye, because ye have no bread? perceive ye not yet, neither understand? have ye your heart hardened? When I brake the five loaves among the five thousand &c.* Hermas addresses the Shepherd in *Mand.* iv., Since the Lord judged me worthy that thou shouldest dwell with me for ever, bear with me for a few words further, because *I understand not at all, and my heart is hardened* by my former doings (2. 1). The combination of *understand not* with the phrase in question points plainly to the Gospels; and

---

* The hardening here spoken of is πώρωσις.

if Hermas took the latter phrase from that source, he must have been acquainted more or less with the accounts of miracles with which it is associated in the Gospels. The phrase being used twice out of three times in S. Mark with allusion to the feeding of the Five Thousand, and so as to include it with other miracles in S. John; this makes it the more likely that *Sim.* v. 2 touches upon that miracle, as we had inferred on other grounds (p. 97). Hardening of heart is spoken of again in *Mand.* xii., Perceivest thou not the glory of God, how great and strong and marvellous it is; in that He created the world for the sake of man, and placed all His creation in subjection to man, and gave him all power to have dominion over all things under heaven? If then, saith he, man is Lord of the creatures of God, and hath dominion over all, the man that hath the Lord in his heart is able to have dominion over these commandments. But *such as have the Lord on their lips, but have their heart hardened and are far from the Lord, to them these commandments are hard and impracticable* (4. 2—4). This brings together widely separated sayings on the lordship of mankind or the Son of man over the creation, as Gen. 1. 28 (κατακυριεύσατε); Psalm 8. 6, with its applications in the New Testament; Matt.

28. 18, *All power is given unto me &c.* As this last is followed by the charge to teach "to observe all things whatsoever I have commanded you," so Hermas passes from man's lordship over the material world to his power to keep the Shepherd's commandments. At the end of the passage from *Mand.* xii. he perhaps refers especially to S. Mark 7. 6—8...*For laying aside the commandment of God &c.*, in connexion with *hardness of heart*, and thus implicitly with the Gospel miracles, which he regards as special signs of the Son of man's lordship over nature. While, for the purposes of his allegory, the writer spiritualises the whole creation and the ideal man's dominion over it, not speaking expressly of any of the miracles as such; he gives sufficient slight indications of acquaintance with the narratives of them in the Gospels.

41] Isaiah saw "his glory," the glory of *Jesus* (ver. 36). On the same principle of Old Testament exegesis it is said in *Epist. Barn.* 12. 7, that in the elevation of the serpent of brass by Moses (Numb. 21. 9) "thou hast again *the glory of Jesus*." Did Barnabas know the Fourth Gospel?* Chap. 21. 2 of the *Epistle*, as von Gebhardt notes, may be based on verse 8, "the poor always ye *have with you*."

* See *The Gospels in the Second Century* by Dr Sanday.

Chap. xiii. 1 *Having loved his own which were in the world, he loved them unto the end.* 4 *He riseth from supper, and...took a towel, and girded himself.* 31 *Now is the Son of man glorified.*

1] Having loved them before, at this crisis He loved them to an extreme, *to the uttermost* (Westcott). This sense of the phrase occurs "most often in connexion with words of destruction." For an example of its use in a different connexion see *Vis.* iii., where the Church on her third appearance is described as of exceeding beauty and *joyous* εἰς τέλος (10. 5).

4—5] The rare word λέντιον, *towel,* is used by Hermas in a context which points to this Gospel, as we shall see under chap. xx. 5 sq. *Gird thyself...and serve me* in *Sim.* viii. 4. 1 is suggestive of S. Luke 17. 8.

31] Here it is said that the Son of man is *glorified*; and the Synoptists speak of his coming *in his glory.* With this agrees the epithet ἔνδοξος given in *Sim.* ix. 12. 8 to the colossal man, the Son of God, whom we identified (pp. 48, 78) with the "Son of man."

Chap. xiv. 2 *In my Father's house are many mansions.* 6 *I am the way, the truth, and the life...no man cometh unto the Father, but by me.* 16 *And I will pray the Father, and he shall give you another Comforter, that he may be with you for ever;* 17 *Even the Spirit of truth...for he abideth with you, and shall be in you.* 20 *Ye in me, and I in you.*

2, 20] The words *dwell, dwelling* are used below for words related to οἰκία, which is rendered "house" in verse 2. In Iren. III. 20. 3 we read, that Christ offered the firstfruits of the resurrection in Himself (1 Cor. 15. 23); that as the Head rose from the dead, so too might all the parts which make up the body, each member having its proper and *fitting** position therein, *For there are many mansions with the Father, since there are also many members in the body.* The writer was thinking of the building of the body of Christ (Eph. 4. 16), to which answers in Hermas the building of the tower. The stones of the tower are fitted variously into the foundation and the walls; and the parallel in the later writer seems to interpret their difference of position as signifying the multiplicity of mansions with the Father. With verse 3, *that where I am, there ye may be also,* compare in *Sim.* ix., And all your seed shall dwell with the Son of God (24. 4).

* Lat. *aptam,* which (as in Iren. V. 36) must stand for ἁρμόζουσαν. This epithet may have been suggested to Irenaeus by the *Shepherd*, in which, from the nature of the subject, ἁρμόζειν is used frequently.

The setting of the stones in the tower represents in a figure, *Ye in me* (ver. 20). Their threefold distinction as inner and outer wall-stones and foundation stones (p. 41) agrees with the threefold difference of dwelling in *Sim.* viii. and Iren. v. 36.

Verse 2 is cited again by Irenaeus, in noteworthy surroundings, at the end of his fifth and last book, thus (v. 36): "As the elders say, That then shall they that are judged worthy to have their abode in heaven go thither, and some shall enjoy the delight of paradise, and others possess *the brightness of the city* (Rev. 21. 23); for everywhere the Saviour shall be seen, *according as they shall be worthy that see him*. And that this is the difference of dwelling of them that bear *the hundred, and the sixty, and the thirty;* of whom the first shall be received up into heaven, and the next abide in paradise, and the last dwell in the city. And that therefore the Lord hath said, *In my Father's (house) are many mansions*. For that all things are of God, who giveth to all their fitting dwelling; as His Word saith, that apportionment hath been made to all by the Father, *according as each is worthy*, or shall be; and that this is the guestchamber in which they shall recline that are invited and feast at the marriage. That this is the *ordering* (1 Cor. 15. 23) and disposition of them that are saved, say the elders the disciples of the Apostles; and that they advance *by such steps*, and ascend through the Spirit to the Son, and through the Son to the Father; the Son at length yielding up his work to the Father, as saith the Apostle, *For he must reign till he put all enemies under his feet &c.* (1 Cor. 15. 25 sq.). Diligently therefore did John foresee the first resurrection of the just." The difference of dwelling of the saved is here connected with the *many mansions* (verse 2); and with the three degrees of success in *the parable of the Sower;* and with *every man in his own order* and other verses of 1 Cor. 15; and seemingly with Rev. 21. 23; and with Matt. 22. 8, which may have suggested "according as they shall be worthy." At any rate this phrase is to be noticed, and likewise "the brightness of the city," for comparison with the parallels in Hermas. Irenaeus rests upon a tradition of the elders, which must have been at least as old as the *Shepherd.* To this we accordingly turn in the hope of finding traces (or further traces) of the tradition therein; and we shall see reason to think that it was well known to Hermas, and was the leading thought of his eighth similitude.

The subject of *Sim.* viii. is a Great Willow, which overspreads the earth, and shelters all who have been called in the name of the Lord. An Angel cuts rods from it, and gives them to the people. Afterwards he demands them back; and they are found to fall into twelve classes, of which the last three are approved. Those of the tenth class were green, as they were first given: those of the eleventh green, and with side-shoots: those of the twelfth green, and with side-shoots, which also had a kind of fruit (1. 1—17). The holders of these last come first, and are crowned and admitted to the tower: those next before them are not crowned, but have entrance to the tower: the next preceding are likewise sent off thither (2. 1—4). This corresponds to "the first resurrection" spoken of in Iren. v. 36. Then the Angel says to the Shepherd, *I go my way* (Joh. 8. 21). Do thou send these others to the walls, *according as any is worthy to dwell*. He accordingly proposes to plant all the rods not approved in the first scrutiny. The holders come in their respective orders*, and he plants their rods, and covers them up with water (as it were *baptizing* them), purposing to come again in a few days, and see if any were alive again, *For he who created this tree* would

---

* Τάγματα τάγματα, the construction from S. Mark 6. 39—40: the word and the idea "every man in his own order" from 1 Cor. 15. 23, which is referred to several times in *Sim.* viii. 4—5.

have all them to live that received branches from it (2. 5—9); the great tree being a figure of the Gospel preached to the whole creation (3. 2). Hermas would know about the *dwelling* of all those who gave up the rods that had been planted (6. 3); and he is told that only those who repent live, for the repentance of sinners hath life and their impenitence death (6. 6); and that the *dwelling* of the saved varies with the character of their repentance (8. 3). Thus in *Sim.* viii. we find the "difference of dwelling" in combination with the three degrees of success in *the parable of the Sower*, to which Hermas alludes here and elsewhere: and likewise with *every man in his own order* and other verses of 1 Cor. 15. But Irenaeus has the same connexion of thought; and he has the phrase *according as each is worthy*, corresponding to *Sim.* viii. 2. 5; and he mentions the *brightness of the city*, which corresponds to the brightness of the tower in *Sim.* ix. 17. 3. It seems to follow that Hermas and Irenaeus were referring to the same tradition of the elders, of which the nucleus was the saying, *In my Father's dwelling are many abodes;* and that Hermas had this saying in mind, although he does not use the word μοναί, *abodes* (Lat. *mansiones*). A later link in the tradition is Tertull. *Scorp.* 6, which connects the *many mansions* with 1 Cor. 15. 41, and with the *steps* of ascent in Iren. v. 36.

In *Sib. Orac.* vii. 68 sq. it is said, that the Word, who had been aforetime maker of earth and starry sky for the Father, became incarnate; and that he quickly flew to the Father's *dwelling* (οἴκους); and that for him were founded *three towers*, to be the abodes of Hope, Piety, Reverence; with allusion (as we must say with Alexandre) to the *Shepherd of Hermas*, in which the oracle somewhere finds the threefold difference of dwelling of the just. Was there anything in Hermas that might be taken to hint at a plurality of towers? In *Vis.* iii. he asks, All these stones that are rejected as not fitting into the building, have they repentance, and shall they find room in this tower? They have repentance, quoth she, *but into this tower they cannot fit; but they shall fit into a different place much smaller* (7. 5—6). The Sibyllist's "maker" is the αὐθέντης who is the Lord of the tower in *Sim.* ix. 5. 6.

6] The actual sayings *I am the way, the truth, the life* are not used in the *Shepherd*, but traces of them may be found there. For *way*, as Zahn suggests, Hermas uses *way-in* (εἴσοδος, 2 Pet. 1. 11) in *Sim.* ix., With these angels the Lord is walled about, and the gate is the Son of God. This is the one way-in to the

Lord. Otherwise shall no one come to Him but through his Son (12. 6). On *the straightness of the Lord*, the straight *way*, see p. 30. Christ, who is the *true light*, and the *true bread*, and the *true vine*, may be referred to in *Vis.* iii. 7. 1 as the *true way* (p. 100). The influence of the saying *I am the truth* is perceptible in *Mand.* iii., *They who lie reject the Lord* (1. 2), in rejecting the truth. The peculiar phrase *deny their life* is a synonym for *deny their Lord* in *Vis.* ii. 2. 7—8. Compare in *Vis.* iii., When thou wast rich thou wast of no use, but now thou art of good use (εὔχρηστος) and serviceable *to the life:* be ye of good use *to God* (6. 7). Remembering the corruption of Christus to *Chrestus* by early heathen writers and the populace, and the ready acceptance of their form of the name as meaning useful and gracious by Justin Martyr and Clement of Alexandria*, we may think that Hermas alludes to "Chrestus" as *the life*.

16—17] On the *Comforter* see below under chap. XVI. 7 sq.

* See Justin *Apol.* I. 4, Whereas we are accused as Christians we are χρηστότατοι... that the χρηστόν should be hated is not just. Clem. *Strom.* II. 4 (p. 438, ed. Potter), Believers on Christ both are and are called χρηστοί: *Cohort.* (ib. p. 72), Ye will not *taste and see*, not that the Lord is χρηστός, as in Psalm 34. 8 (1 Pet. 2. 3), but *that Christ is God*.

Chap. xv. 1 *I am the true vine, and my Father is the husbandman. 2 Every branch that beareth fruit, he purgeth it, that it may bring forth more fruit. 5 I am the vine, ye are the branches.*

The Son of God makes himself the ideal vine, with implicit allusion to parables of the Old Testament, such as Psalm 80. 8—10, *Thou broughtest a vine out of Egypt...it filled the land. The hills were covered with the shadow of it.* Hermas, after his manner, changes the form of the parable, and speaks in *Sim.* viii. of a great Willow covering hills and mountains (1. 1). This luxuriant tree, which covers the whole earth, is the law of God given to all the world, which law is *the Son of God* preached to the ends of the earth (3. 2). The tree's singular vitality expresses that its Creator would have all live that have received branches from it (2. 7, 9). These branches are cut from it by an Angel and given by him to the people under its shelter, who had been called in the name of the Lord (1. 2); and the spiritual status of the recipients is represented by their branches or rods as they give them back, some dry, some flourishing in various degrees (6. 4 sq.). This is the writer's way of saying, *Ye are the branches.* To the husbandman's care for every branch of the True Vine corresponds the planting (Matt. 15. 13) and watering of all the willow rods that were withered or faulty when first given up, in the hope that they may revive (2. 6). Thus in *Sim.* viii. we have all the elements of the parable of the Vine and its Branches. The fruit of the true vine is "fruit of truth" (*Sim.* ix. 19. 2).

Chap. xvi. 1 *These things have I spoken unto you, that ye should not be offended.* 5 *And none of you asketh me, Whither goest thou?* 7 *It is expedient for you that I go away: for if I go not away, the Comforter will not come unto you; but if I depart, I will send him unto you.* 8 *And when he is come, he will convict the world of sin.* 12 *I have yet many things to say unto you, but ye cannot bear them now.* 13 *Howbeit when he, the Spirit of truth, is come, he will guide you into all truth: for he shall not speak of himself.* 16 *A little while, and ye shall not see me: and again, a little while, and ye shall see me.* 20 *And ye shall be sorrowful &c.* 26 *And I say not unto you, that I will pray the Father for you.* 32 *And yet I am not alone, because the Father is with me.*

1, 5, 12] The word *be offended* (ver. 1), which would have been suggested by the Gospels, is used in *Vis.* iv., And give repentance to all the servants of God that have *been offended*, that His great and glorious name may be glorified (1. 3); and *Mand.* viii. 10, Not to cast away them that have *been offended* from the faith. In verse 5 the disciples are reproached for not asking a question, as elsewhere for asking. So Hermas (cf. p. 40), to whom the Shepherd says at the end of *Sim.* ix., Wherefore didst thou not ask me concerning *the print of the stones* placed in the building, how that we filled up the prints? On the principle that vocabulary is an indication of an author's literary sources, and on other grounds, the conjecture may be hazarded that Hermas knew the phrase *print of the nails* in chap. xx. 25. The words for *print...prints* in the passage cited, which is extant only in Latin, are *forma...formas;* but the previous passage to which it refers gives the Greek τοὺς τύπους τῶν λίθων (10. 1—2). With verse 12, *but ye cannot bear now* what I have to say, compare in *Vis.* i. 3. 3, *words which a man cannot bear* (βαστάσαι), and *Sim.* ix. 1. 2.

7—8, 13] The Spirit of truth is spoken of in chap. xiv. 17 as dwelling and being "with you" and "in you," and so in *Mand.* iii. 1, 4: in chap. xv. 26 as proceeding from the Father: and in 1 Joh. 4. 6 in contrast with the spirit of error. With the phrase *convict of sin* (ver. 8) compare in *Vis.* i., I was taken up that I might *convict thy sins* unto the Lord (1. 5). Hermas, who usually presents his leading ideas under more than one aspect, makes the Shepherd, the angel of repentance, as well as the twelve virgins, correspond more or less to the Paraclete*, who is to "abide with you for ever" (Joh. 14. 16). This angel says in *Vis.* v. 2, "I am sent by the most reverend Angel to dwell with thee the remaining days of thy life." And in *Sim.* ix. 1. 3 he says, "Thou must from me *learn all things* more exactly, for to this end was I given by the glorious Angel to dwell in thine house;" where *learn all things* answers to "he shall teach you all things" (Joh. 14. 26). The thought of the Spirit dwelling with a man enters into the version of the Two Ways in *Mand.* vi., where Hermas asks how he is to know whether the two angels, of Righteousness and Wickedness, are dwelling with him (2. 2). The twelve virgins, likewise, if they denote the Holy Spirit, should satisfy the condition of being sent to dwell with the faithful; who, without the aid of the divine Spirit cannot keep the commandments of God. This condition they fully satisfy,

* But there are two Paracletes. *We have a Paraclete with the Father, Jesus Christ* (1 Joh. 2. 1), who says, *I will come to you* (Joh. 14. 18), *I am with you alway* (Matt. 28. 20); and the Spirit of truth is promised as "another Paraclete" (Joh. 14. 16).

for in *Sim.* ix., before the vigil by the tower, they say to Hermas, Thou art our brother, and henceforth we shall dwell with thee (11. 3); and it is said that their spirits remained with and never departed from the foundation stones (15. 6). And in *Sim.* x. the superior Angel counsels Hermas to keep the commandments of the Shepherd, and sends him the virgins for his spiritual direction, saying, "I have sent thee these virgins to dwell with thee; for I have seen that they are courteous unto thee. Thou hast them therefore as helpers, that thou mayest the better keep his commandments; for *without these virgins it is not possible that they should be kept.* I see that they like to be with thee; but I will command them that they depart not at all from thy house. Only do thou cleanse thy house, for in a cleanly house they like to dwell.... When he had thus said, he gave me again in charge to the Shepherd, and called the virgins, and said unto them, Seeing that ye like to dwell in this man's house, I commend him and his house to you, that ye depart not at all from his house" (2—3). The similitude (and with it the whole work) ends somewhat strangely as follows, *When the Angel had done speaking with me, he arose from the bed, and took the Shepherd and the virgins and departed; saying however to me that he would send back the Shepherd and the virgins to my house.* The departure and the promise are explained by the promise (Luke 24. 49) of the Comforter, *But if I depart, I will send him unto you* (Joh. 16. 7). The Spirit of truth shall not *speak of himself* (ver. 13): the true prophet in *Mand.* xi. 5 *speaks all things of himself*, in the sense that "whatsoever he shall hear, that shall he speak," unlike the deceiver who waits to be enquired of by men, that he may prophesy according to their desires.

16—19, 32] The saying *A little while &c.* is emphasised by repetition and pressed upon the attention of the reader, the word μικρόν, *a little while*, occurring seven times in ver. 16—19. Accordingly in *Sim.* ix., when the visitation of the Lord of the tower is being prepared for, the Shepherd in reply to the demand of Hermas for explanation of what had been shewn him, takes the word up and says, *A little while* I am preoccupied, after which I will explain all things: wait for me here *till I come.* I say to him, Sir, *alone* here what should I do? Thou art *not* (saith he) *alone, because these virgins are with thee* (10. 5—6). *Not alone* (ver. 32), because of the invisible presence of these virgins, who are (as we have seen) the Holy Spirit. Of a piece with this is the objective rendering of *Men loved darkness rather than light* (Joh. 3. 19) in *Sim.* ix. 13. 8, They loved (ἐπεθύμησαν) the women in black [9. 5], and put on their power, and put off the raiment or power of the virgins.

20—22] *And ye shall be sorrowful, but your sorrow shall be turned into joy. A woman when she is in travail hath sorrow, because her hour is come: but as soon as she is delivered of the child, she remembereth no more the anguish, for joy that a man is born into the world. And ye now therefore have sorrow: but I will see you again, and your heart shall rejoice, and your joy no man taketh from you.* Hermas in *Vis.* iii. 13 (p. 8), "For as when to one sorrowing come *good tidings* he straightway forgetteth the former sorrows... so ye too have received renewal of your spirits &c.", seems to be adapting these verses to the case of the Church personified, whereof "ye" the persons addressed are members. For the figure of birth in verse 21 he has new birth of the spirit. His word ἀγγελία, *tidings*, is from 1 Joh. 1. 5 and 3. 11, the only occurrences of the word in the New Testament. He further disguises the reference to the Gospel by writing *straightway forgetteth* (Jas. 1. 24) for "remembereth no more." On the other hand, when in *Vis.* i. 3. 3 the Church says to Hermas, γενοῦ ἀκροατής, *be a hearer*, and when he proves a "forgetful hearer" (Jas. 1. 25), this is expressed as a not remembering, so as to disguise the allusion to S. James. Notice the play upon the "law of liberty" (Jas. 1. 25) in *Sim.* v. 2. 2, *Keep this my commandment, and thou shalt be free.*

    · The personification of the Church in the *Shepherd* is of a very real and dramatic kind. On occasion indeed she betrays her corporate character, but in general her individuality is well marked and lifelike: she converses with Hermas, addresses him by name, gives him a book to read and copy: he calls her *Lady*, would have her seated before him (*Vis.* iii. 1. 8), prays her by the Lord to shew him the promised vision (2. 3), mistakes her identity at first (ii. 4. 1), perhaps on the suggestion of chap. xx. 14. Is she the *Elect Lady* of the Second Epistle of S. John? This Lady has *children;* and the Church addresses her *children* in *Vis.* iii. 9. 1. The "elect" of God are spoken of by Hermas in *Vis.* i. ii. iii. iv. only (Hilgf.). S. John prays the Lady "that we may love one another" (ver. 5); where and in verse 13 she is addressed as *thee*, but "in the intermediate verses the plural is used." Granted of her that, as Bp Westcott decides, "No interpretation can be accepted as satisfactory," the allegorist (who was free to choose the sense which best served his purpose) has made his Lady the Church correspond in outline to the Elect Lady of S. John.

26] On *pray the Father for you* Bp Westcott writes, "This use of *ask* (ἐρωτᾷν) in connexion with prayer addressed to God is peculiar to St John." Notice its use in 1 Joh. 5. 16, "There is a *sin* unto death: I do not say that he shall *pray for* it;" comparing in *Vis.* iii., Hermas, cease *praying* always *for thy sins:* pray for righteousness also (1. 6). All *prayer*, says the Church, requires humility: fast therefore and thou shalt receive what thou askest from the Lord (10. 6). *Pray the Lord that* thou mayest receive understanding &c. (*Sim.* ix. 2. 6).

Chap. xvii. 1 *Father...glorify thy Son.* 2 *As thou hast given him power over all flesh, that he should give eternal life to as many as thou hast given him.* 4 *I have finished the work which thou gavest me to do.* 5 *Glorify thou me with thine own self with the glory which I had with thee before the world was.* 8 *I have given unto them the words which thou gavest me.* 12 *While I was with them in the world, I kept them in thy name: those that thou gavest me I have kept.* 21 *That they all may be one &c.* 24 *Thou lovedst me before the foundation of the world.*

1—12, 24] Returning to the parable of the Vineyard we read in *Sim.* v. 6. 2—5, God planted the vineyard, that is created the people, and *gave* them in charge (παρέδωκεν) to His Son (ver. 12); and the Son set the angels over them to *keep** them, and... having Himself cleansed their sins, *shewed* them the paths of life [Ps. 16. 11], having given them the law which He received from His Father (ver. 8). Thou seest, saith he, that He is Lord of the people, *having received all power from His Father*. Now, that the Lord took counsel with His Son and the glorious angels, hearken, *The preexistent Holy Spirit &c.* (p. 73). The bestowal of all power [Matt. 28. 18] *by the Father* points to ver. 1—2; where moreover the purpose of the gift is said to be that the Son should give eternal life to those given to Him. His so doing is expressed above in terms of the Old Testament, except that ἔδειξεν, *shewed*, may be from chap. xiv. 6—8†, *I am the way...shew us the Father*. The promise to the slave that he should be free παρ'

---

* Συντηρεῖν, a word of the Synoptists, for τηρεῖν (ver. 12).

† With *We know not whither thou goest* (xiv. 5) compare the ending of *Vis.* iv., and in *Vis.* i. 4. 3 ὑπάγουσα. The word ὑπάγειν is used about 80 times in the Synoptic and Johannine writings and but once besides (Jas. 2. 16) in the New Testament. It is used in Joh. 3. 8 of the going of the πνεῦμα, and in *Vis.* iii. 5. 3 and *Sim.* ix. 3. 3 of the going of the unhewn stones (p. 30), which are they that are "born of the Spirit."

ἐμοί, *with me* (2. 2), after *finishing* his task (2. 4), is a promise of the fellowship with the Father after finished work prayed for in verse 5, *with thyself...with thee*. The thought that the Son was temporarily in the world and had charge in it of men gathered from it (ver. 6—13) is obliquely but definitely expressed by the placing of the slave in and in charge of the vineyard, which was planted in a portion of *the field* (2. 2), which *is this world* (5. 2), and by his eventual transference to a higher sphere. The passages of the *Shepherd* on the preexistence of Christ may be assumed to comprise a reference to His sayings, *before the world was...before the foundation of the world &c.* (ver. 5, 24). Notice the *I am &c.* of the Church (*Vis.* iii. 3. 3), the beginning of the creation of God (ii. 4. 1), who as represented by the tower contains the generations (p. 11) before Abraham (Joh. 8. 58).

21] The unification of believers is a distinct feature of the allegory of Hermas. In *Vis.* iii. he says, The stones did so cleave to one another that no join could be seen; but the building of the tower was as if it were built of one stone (2. 6). *Sim.* ix. further expresses their oneness with the rock, Christ, For the tower was so built as if of one stone not having a single join in it. The stone looked as if hewn out of the rock; for it seemed a monolith unto me (9. 7). And again, Therefore thou seest the tower as become *monolith with the rock*. Thus also they that have believed upon the Lord through His Son, and that put on these spirits, shall become one spirit, one body, and their garments of one colour (13. 5).

Chap. xviii. 27 *Peter denied again.*

Three of the Gospels record that Peter *denied again*, and none uses the phrase in any other connexion. It is found in the remarkable passage of *Vis.* ii., Thou shalt say to Maximus, Behold affliction cometh. If it seem good to thee, *deny again*. The Lord is nigh unto them that turn to Him; as it is written in Eldad and Modat, who prophesied in the wilderness to the people (3. 4). The name of Maximus, whether a real personage or not, would serve to mask an allusion to the chiefest of the Apostles. The writer says satirically, *Deny again*, if it seem good to thee, and repent when the trial is over; trusting to the assurance of those prophets of the people that the Lord is always nigh unto them that turn to Him. *Mand.* iv. 3. 6 allows but one repentance, and condemns those who go on sinning and repenting. The doubleminded or doubtful repent frequently

(*Mand.* xi. 4). "O thou of little faith, wherefore didst thou doubt?"

Chap. xix. 1 *Then Pilate therefore took Jesus, and scourged him.* 11 *Thou couldest have no power...except it were given thee from above.* 13 *Pilate...brought Jesus forth, and sat down in the judgment seat.* 23 *Now the coat was without seam, woven from the top throughout.* 24 *They said therefore among themselves, Let us not rend it.*

1, 11] This *scourging* is implied, on the same principle as the Crucifixion, by the Church's claim to sit upon the right hand (p. 51). Scourge may mean *plague* also, as in Mark 3. 10; and the Church in *Vis.* iv. says that the Almighty is able to send *plagues* upon the doubleminded (2. 6). The *scourge* of the angel of retribution (*Sim.* vi. 2. 5) reminds of the *flagellum* [Matt. 27. 26] of chap. ii. 15; and for the term "house" (ii. 16) we may quote from *Sim.* ix., *they remained in the house of God* (13. 9)...*they shall not enter into the house of God* (14. 1), comparing Matt. 12. 4 for the words of the latter saying, and Joh. 8. 35 for the idea of the former. That *authority* and power are *from above* (ver. 11) is illustrated by the force of dropping water and hail in *Mand.* xi. (p. 82).

13] Pilate *sat down:* or he *caused* Jesus *to sit down,* "completing in this way the scene of the 'Ecce Homo' by shewing the King on His throne." The action may not seem to fall in with the position of a Roman governor (Westcott), and New Testament analogy may favour the intransitive rendering; but the other sense, though it be not the true one, is grammatically possible, as in *Vis.* iii. 2. 4, where the Church *seats* (καθίζει) Hermas upon the bench. Attention has been called recently* to the apparent acceptance of the transitive rendering by Justin Martyr, who relates in *Apol.* I. 35, as a fulfilment of prophecy, that *the Jews in derision set* Jesus Christ *upon a judgment seat* (ἐκάθισαν ἐπὶ βήματος), *and said, Judge for us* [Luke 12. 14]. It may have been his policy not to implicate Pilate, but he refers to the *Acts of Pilate.* In the case of the woman taken in adultery (p. 100), we read in *Apost. Const.* II. 24 that the elders devolved *the judgment* upon Jesus.

23—24] Hermas, who lays stress upon the tower being without apparent join, would have noticed the sayings, *The coat was without seam…Let us not rend it;* and he has himself a parable of a garment in *Sim.* ix. 32, Amend therefore while yet the tower

* By Dr Drummond, cited by Salmon, *Introd. to N. T. Lect.* 6.

is being built. The Lord dwelleth in men that love peace......Give back to Him therefore a spirit whole as ye received it. For if thou shouldest have given a new sound garment to a fuller, and he return it rent, wilt thou not be at once angry, and reproach him?...And what thinkest thou the Lord will do to thee, who gave thee a spirit unimpaired, which thou hast altogether spoiled? Some Latin Fathers make the unrent "coat" of Christ emblematic of the Church in its unity (Wordsworth). S. Cyprian in *De Unit. Eccl.* 7 (contrasting 1 Kings 11. 30 sq.) says that it represents the close concord of such as have put on Christ, which those who rend the Church cannot do; and it may be that Hermas was his forerunner in this comparison. He makes a mystery of the "coats" of the virgins, which they *spread* (Matt. 21. 8) on the ground under him in *Sim.* ix. 11. 7. It would have been nothing strange in such a writer to teach that, as the *chiton* of Christ was not to be rent, so His disciples should endeavour to keep the unity of the Spirit in the bond of peace (13. 5. viii. 2. 3); but what could possibly have led him to think in this connexion of a garment given to a fuller to be scoured? In one place only of the New Testament the word fuller is found, and there it is said that no "fuller" on earth could whiten the glistering garments *of Jesus* (p. 37).

Chap. xx. 5 *And he stooping down, and looking in, saw the linen clothes lying; yet went he not in.* 6 *Then cometh Simon Peter following him, and went into the sepulchre, and seeth the linen clothes lie,* 7 *And the napkin, that was about his head, not lying with the linen clothes.* 9 *As yet they knew not the scripture.*

5—7] Hermas, awaiting the apparition of the Church, says, "I see an ivory bench *lying*, and upon the bench *lay* a linen bolster, and over it a linen *towel* (Joh. 13. 4) of fine flax spread out. Seeing these *lying*, and no one in the place, I became affrighted (ἔκθαμβος) &c." (*Vis.* iii. 1. 4—5). The description of these things *lying*, and no one in the place, points to the Evangelist's impressive description of the linen clothes *lying* in the vacant sepulchre. The occasions also correspond, for the previous visions had pictured the death and resurrection of the Church.

9] While to Hermas in his visions there is no Scripture but what he writes down on the authority of the Church (*Vis.* ii. 4. 3) or of the Shepherd (v. 6), he gives us side-glances at the Scriptures properly so called, and uses his own record of the revelation to himself as a symbol of them. The Shepherd does not say to him, *Search the scriptures* (p. 95), but instructs him to read his draft of the mandates and similitudes without intermission (v. 5). The Church lends him a booklet, written antiquely without division into words, so that he can only copy it letter for letter without understanding it (ii. 1. 4); but fifteen days later, after much fasting and prayer, he has *the knowledge of the writing* revealed to him, and he tells us what were the *things-written* (2. 1). This *gnosis* of the Scripture, which is a gift that cometh from above, is what the disciples lacked when *as yet they knew not the scripture* (ver. 9), which their mind was afterwards opened to understand (Luke 24. 45). In like manner, when we read in *Sim.* v. 3. 7 that Hermas must *quite-accomplish* [Mark 13. 4] *the things written*, this is a reminder of the saying in Luke 18. 31, *All the things written by the prophets concerning the Son of man shall be accomplished.*

Chap. xxi. 18 *Thou shalt stretch forth thy hands, and another shall gird thee.* 19 *This spake he, signifying by what death he should glorify God.* 25 *And there are also many other things which Jesus did, the which, if they should be written every one, I suppose that even the world itself could not contain the books that should be written.*

18] Tradition says that S. Peter was crucified with his head downwards, and verse 18 is commonly thought to point to the *extension* of his hands upon the Cross. Some demur to this: but it matters little for our purpose what *stretch forth* originally meant, if only by the time of Hermas it had come to be applied to the Apostle's crucifixion. If Hermas, as we may assume, took it in that sense, it would help to account for his making his dragon of tribulation *stretch itself forth* upon the ground, with allusion to the sign of the Cross. The transition from man to beast might be thought to be a difficulty. But Justin Martyr writes that the mystery of the Paschal Lamb was a type of Christ (*Dial.* 40), for other reasons and because it was, as it were, crucified, one spit traversing the length of its body, and the other going through it crosswise, to which the *hands of the lamb* were attached. Thus he sees the Crucifixion in the stretching out of what he calls the "hands of the lamb."

25] *Sim.* ix. 2. 1 shews the reverse side of this last word of the Fourth Gospel by making the rock, the Son of God, *able to contain the whole world.*

The evidence adduced seems to justify the conclusion that the Gospel known to Hermas was (so to say) a Diatessaron, having for its elements the Four Gospels of to-day. The reader who would carry the investigation further will find a revised text and a translation of the *Shepherd* by Mr J. R. Harmer, in the late Bishop of Durham's posthumous second work upon *The Apostolic Fathers* (1891).

The foregoing argument is not opposed but supplementary to the reasoning which has led some writers on Hermas and the Gospels to an opposite conclusion. It has scarcely been denied that there are on the one hand appearances of a use of the Gospels, and on the other hand *nulla certa vestigia*, no indubitable traces of them, in the *Shepherd*; and this has left its readers the option of inferring with more or less hesitation that the writer knew the Gospels, or affirming with greater or less assurance that there is or may be some better explanation of his apparent allusions to them. In all this no account had been taken of the saying, *For the world also is compacted of four elements*, which sets the seal to the revelation to Hermas in *Vis*. iii. But it was natural in one who wrote as Hermas wrote to hint at the *Evangelium* as *Good Tidings*; and when this thin disguise was seen through, Irenaeus completed the interpretation of the oracle, as is shewn above in the *Preface* and in the chapter on *Hermas and the Four Gospels*. The interpretation is simple and adequate, and when rightly approached obvious, and there is not, so far as I have observed, any other.

The details of the "witness" of Hermas in the subsequent chapters are not meant to stand alone as proofs of his literary use of the Gospels, but to be taken with and as verifications of the antecedent general proof that he accepted them; for which we are entitled to claim validity until reason has been shewn to the contrary. Of such verifications perhaps the most convincing are some which are neither verbal nor upon the surface, as those which postulate the representation of the Holy Ghost by a catena of personified fruits of the Spirit from Faith to Love. That this was intended, Hermas tells us with comparative plainness of speech; and the identification of "these spirits" and the Spirit was gradually found to lighten one dark place after another*. I would add now that

---

* This identification was accepted in the first instance on the suggestion of words of Hermas, and was found to bear the test of application to a number of passages which were obscure without it. Some of these

Hermas may have known the saying of Ignatius that Faith and Love in one are God (*Eph.* 14).

The *Shepherd* has lately engaged the attention of the learned author of the *Agrapha* (p. 105), who has compiled a long list of references thereto in part preparation for a general collection of extra-canonical parallels to the Gospels. Of these references, the majority of which are to the Synoptic Gospels, it is interesting to notice that some are to the last twelve verses of S. Mark. In corroboration of the proof from his own writings that Justin Martyr knew them (p. 67), it is to be remarked that his disciple Tatian, according to Professor Hemphill's account of his work (1888), used a part or the whole of every one of the twelve as material for his composite Gospel the *Diatessaron*.

applications may or may not be new; but the identification of the many spirits with the One is to be found in the scanty but choice notes on the *Shepherd* in the anonymous Oxford *Barnabas and Hermas* of 1685 [Bp Fell], and in quotations of them by Le Clerc and later writers. Fell quotes Cotelier's reference on "sabano" in the Latin of *Sim.* viii. 4. 1 (p. 120) to Clem. Alex. *Paed.* II. 3, where it is said that Jesus girded Himself σαβάνῳ [for λεντίῳ].

THE END.

www.ingramcontent.com/pod-product-compliance
Lightning Source LLC
Chambersburg PA
CBHW030318170426
43202CB00009B/1055